The Andaman Islanders

THE AUTHOR

Lidio Cipriani was Professor of Anthropology at the University of Florence until his death in October, 1962. *The Andaman Islanders* was the last major project which he completed, and one with which he was deeply concerned. Professor Cipriani had spent many months in the Andaman Islands, and his research among these peoples was particularly well known to anthropologists through his many papers to learned journals.

LIDIO CIPRIANI

The Andaman Islanders

Edited and translated by
D. TAYLER COX
assisted by LINDA COLE

FREDERICK A. PRAEGER, *Publishers*
New York · Washington

BOOKS THAT MATTER

Published in the United States of America in 1966
by Frederick A. Praeger, Inc., Publishers
111 Fourth Avenue, New York 3, N.Y.

All rights reserved
© 1966 by Lidio Cipriani
English translation © 1966 by George Weidenfeld and
Nicolson, Ltd., London, England

Library of Congress Catalog Card Number: 66-20312

Printed in Great Britain

Contents

Illustrations

Editor's Note

The editing and publication of any posthumous work is inevitably a difficult task, and the preparation of the present volume has been made the more so as the material came into our hands only after Professor Cipriani's death, and was clearly intended to become a final expression of his scientific and philosophical experience.

Among the readers of this book there may be scientists who will deplore on principle any attempt to present scientific observations in a form attractive to the general reader. Happily, their numbers are dwindling rapidly, and we make no apology for trying to bring to as wide a public as possible observations which, quite apart from any intrinsic scientific value, may help in some measure to remedy the paucity of material so far published on the peoples of the Andaman Islands, and stimulate the further research which Cipriani himself felt to be so urgently needed.

On going through the mass of data left by Professor Cipriani it became abundantly clear that not only did he intend the scientific matter to be published in detail in various scientific journals, but that this resumé of his observations was intended to be a framework within which he hoped to set out the views to which he had been led by his experiences as an anthropologist over a period of many years. It was equally clear that not everyone would feel in sympathy with these views, and the philosophy which they express. While, therefore, there is no doubt that Professor Cipriani would have been fully able and prepared to support them scientifically, I have not felt competent to do so, nor, frankly, would I feel it my province as a layman to engage in controversy over 'big bang' and 'steady state' theories of evolution. The present volume, therefore, does not and cannot claim to be other than a record of the late Professor Cipriani's observations and experiences in the Andamans, and as such let it be judged.

Foreword

The following pages represent a brief account of my observations during a period of nearly two years which I spent in the Andaman Islands, living for part of the time with the Onges, who provide the major part of my material.

I had for a long time been interested in the vexed question of the origins of the pygmies, and after spending some years studying them in Africa and in Asia I came to the conclusion that the peoples of the Andaman archipelago might well represent the 'purest' living example of Negrito stock and culture, remaining as they have in complete isolation until very recently. After a brief visit to the Islands in 1951, therefore, and with the warm co-operation of all the officials and government departments concerned, I was able, beginning in 1952, to spend a total of 634 days in the Islands, 162 of them living in the forests of Little Andaman with the Onges.

It would be impossible to list individually the Indian government officials who aided me in every way, but I wish to record here my deepest appreciation of the courtesy and help extended to me by all the departments and individuals with whom I had dealings, both in the Andamans and in India itself. To all of them, whatever their rank or station, are due my warmest thanks – without their help these notes, incomplete as they are, could never have been written.

Armed with gifts of mirrors, glass beads, cloth and, above all, tobacco, I was able to make friends with the reputedly ferocious people of the Andamans and to make observations which, though but a beginning, will I hope lead others to carry further the work which I was able to begin. During my visits to the Islands I was able to set up a museum at Port Blair, where I hope ultimately to build up a complete picture of the life and culture of the islanders; it will fall to others to continue where I have had to stop, and I can only hope, in these pages, to awaken in others the interest and sympathy which I came to feel for these strange, child-like, but lovable people – the Onges of Little Andaman.

LIDIO CIPRIANI

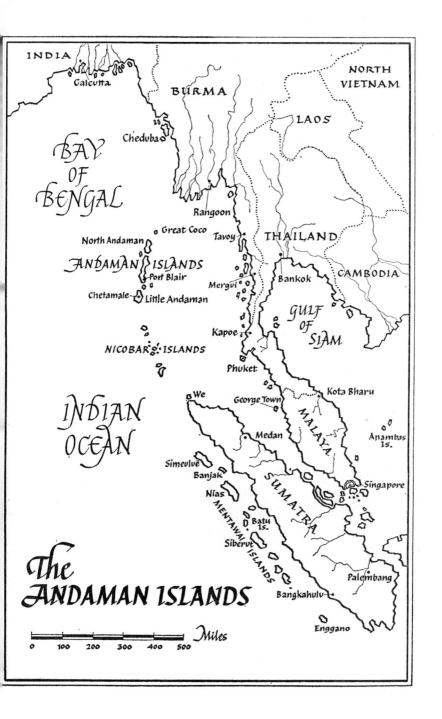

INDIA

Calcutta

BURMA

NORTH
VIETNAM

LAOS

Cheduba

BAY
OF
BENGAL

Rangoon

Great Coco

Tavoy

THAILAND

North Andaman

ANDAMAN ISLANDS

CAMBODIA

Port Blair

Mergui

Bankok

Chetamale — Little Andaman

GULF
OF
SIAM

Kapoe

NICOBAR ISLANDS

Phuket

INDIAN
OCEAN

We

Kota Bharu

George Town

MALAYA

Medan

Anambas
Is.

Simeulue

Banjak

SUMATRA

Singapore

Nias

MENTAWAI ISLANDS

Batu
Is.

The
ANDAMAN ISLANDS

Siberut

Palembang

Bangkahulu

Miles

0   100   200   300   400   500

Enggano

CHAPTER ONE

The People of the Islands

In the Bay of Bengal, eight hundred miles to the south-east of Calcutta and a hundred and twenty miles from Cape Nigrais in Burma, the two hundred and four islands of the Andaman archipelago stretch out in a line, with a surface area of 6,495 square kilometres. To the south-east, about a hundred miles away, lie the Nicobars, strung out in a much smaller chain covering only 1,645 square kilometres and made up of twenty-one islands, of which only twelve are inhabited.

The only islands in the Andamans which are permanently occupied are Great Andaman and Little Andaman. The former, three hundred and twenty kilometres long and at no point more than forty kilometres wide, was broken up by geological movement in ancient times into three sections, known as North, South and Middle Andaman. Today these are separated from each other by two narrow straits hardly navigable even by vessels of low tonnage. A much larger passage, the Ten Degree Channel, so called because it is crossed by the 10° north parallel, separates the Andamans from the Nicobars, and incidentally forms a dividing line between ordinarily different worlds, worlds which in the past, as I hope to show, had many characteristics in common.

The Nicobars are peopled by a very ancient Mongoloid race. There are no foreigners permanently resident apart from a family of Moslem merchants from India with a few employees. There are also the Shom-Pen, a small, wild and semi-nomadic group who have been forced back into the forests of Great Nicobar, where they preserve their ancient somatic and cultural characteristics, showing affinities with a Mongoloid people living far away on the chain of islands off the west coast of Sumatra.

The population of the Andamans, on the other hand, is now almost entirely of recent immigration: there are no Europeans permanently resident, but a large number of colonists of Indian, Burmese or Malayan origin have made their home in the islands. In the Indian census of 1951, the entire stable population of the Andamans and Nicobars was assessed at thirty thousand, 18,962 in the Andamans and 12,009 in the Nicobars, not counting the Shom-Pen. The few aboriginals remaining in the Andamans are anthropologically of extreme importance. Classified among the Negritos, or Asiatic pygmies, they are one of the few surviving groups of pygmies who in the past were widely scattered all over the world. They can be divided into three groups, clearly distinguished one from the other by their mode of life, their present genetic isolation (although they certainly all originated from a common stock) and their attitude towards outsiders:

1 The Arioto, the friendly Andamanese, once very numerous along the coast of Great Andaman and now reduced to only twenty-three individuals of pure stock; now almost completely sterile, they are near to extinction. They manage to survive only because of the help given to them by the Indian Government, which has established small camps along the coasts of Middle Andaman.

2 The Jarawas, still implacably hostile to foreigners, living a nomadic existence in South and Middle Andaman. One solitary group occupies a tiny island thirty miles west of South Andaman, surrounded by seas so stormy that they are frequently impassable. This is known as North Sentinel, to distinguish it from South Sentinel, twenty miles to the south and uninhabited. Landing on North Sentinel, as indeed penetrating anywhere on Great Andaman, has hitherto always entailed vicious fighting with the Jarawas, who are determined to repulse any stranger from their last refuge. They are well sheltered by an unbelievably dense forest, which has so far made it impossible to subdue them, though there are today probably no more than two hundred surviving.

3 The Onges, sole inhabitants of Little Andaman, into which they have withdrawn. There are not more than five hundred surviving today, and these are in a state of serious demographic decline. It is probable that before 1952 no one had ever approached their camps in the interior of the island. Until the present day, they

have always been protected by the sea, which is almost invariably rough, and by a thick tropical forest which extends without a break over more than a thousand square kilometres, unpenetrated by outsiders and almost impenetrable.

THE ARIOTO

The decline of the Andamanese began with the first landing of foreigners on the island and is similar to that of so many other primitive peoples who have come into contact with civilization; a detailed account of their decline would be long and pitiful. In the case of the Andamanese, however, demographic influences arising thousands of years ago must also be taken into account. Cut off by circumstances into small groups and separated at random by large expanses of sea or by the impenetrable forest, they gradually developed somatic and cultural differences of the greatest scientific interest. Among other things, languages became modified to such an extent that members of different groups are unable to understand one another. The Onges, for example, who in my opinion are the nearest relations of the Jarawas, are quite unable to understand their language.

The peoples of Great Andaman were the first to encounter civilization, when from 1858 onwards the Indian Government, then in English hands, decided to institute at Port Blair a penitentiary for the many political prisoners after the famous 1857 mutiny. Subsequently the government sent over convicts serving long or life sentences. The life of the deportees was atrocious during the first few years, owing to malaria and the absence of medical supplies. To the majority, therefore, deportation to the Andamans meant a death sentence. Even today the only large brick building in the Andamans and Nicobars is the penitentiary at Port Blair.

Before the building of the penitentiary the English had made several desultory expeditions to the Andamans, and even before then other foreigners had landed on the archipelago. It is known that Marco Polo, probably passing within sight of the archipelago in 1292, gave it the name of Angaman, and declared the inhabitants to be ferocious cannibals with dogs' heads. As a result, even the Asian pirates were for centuries afraid to land on the islands. The barbarous forays of Arab slave traders later awoke in the islanders a furious aversion to foreigners. This hatred has been rekindled during the last hundred years by a number of unfortunate incidents, but at one time the islanders were favourably disposed towards seafarers passing by, if we are to believe Niccolo dei Conti and Cesare Federici, fleeting visitors to the islands in 1440 and 1569. They both wrote of the peaceful native canoes that approached their ships, and this is confirmed by other travellers, like the Italians Fra Odorico da Pordenone in 1332 and Giovan Francesco Gemelli Caresi in 1709.

Violent clashes with the coastal tribes only became frequent when the English began to take an interest in the Andamans as a possible penal colony. The first prisoners to be sent there were some Indians, in 1788. In 1796 the colony was abolished owing to the swift death of nearly all the prisoners from tropical diseases. The attempt was repeated in 1858 after a mission entrusted to F. Mouat, and this time the seeds of decline for the islanders were sown. Efforts were begun to approach the coastal peoples, and even, strangely enough, those of the forests, the now ferocious Jarawas. Some of these tentative overtures were well received, but once the islanders came to think they had been betrayed it was enough to rekindle the hatred of strangers which they have retained ever since.

The evidence obtainable from archaeological excavations shows that for thousands of years the people encountered by the English in the coastal areas were the sole inhabitants of Great Andaman, living by fishing rather than by hunting or cultivation in the forests. The Jarawas arrived later. Migration from Little Andaman, imposed in relatively recent times by lack of food, brought them to Great Andaman. Since the entire coastal region was already occupied, the new arrivals took refuge in the forests of the hinterland. There they were happy, for they found an abundance of wild honey and fruit which amply fulfilled their needs. A spontaneous equilibrium was established between the coast-people and the forest-people, and both prospered.

The arrival of an appreciable number of foreigners in 1858 immediately changed the situation. The peoples of the coast, who were the most anxious to make friends with the strangers, paid for this fatal error with virtual extermination. When the foreigners had definitely established themselves, the coastal Andamanese – *Arioto*

4

in the local language, as opposed to the people of the interior, the *Eremtaga* – appear to have numbered between six and eight thousand. Over the years their place has been taken by more than thirteen thousand foreigners, most of whom were deportees, enjoying relative liberty as servants of government officials, farmers and foresters. The settlers, voluntarily or involuntarily, introduced the islanders to alcohol and tobacco, forcing them to turn to the foreigners in order to satisfy their craving. In the famous and extremely frank work of the English explorer M. V. Portman (*A History of our Relations with the Andamanese*, Calcutta, 1899) official letters are reproduced which give precise instructions in the matter to government officials. The result of these instructions was to transform the Arioto into alcohol and tobacco addicts. Syphilis was passed to the native women by the deportees, and from them to their men. When, a few years after the mass importation of prisoners, the government authorities became aware of the infection among the Arioto, not one of them had escaped. The miserable twenty-three survivors of the eight to nine thousand of a century ago show the ultimate result only too well, and their final extinction is imminent.

Before the advent of the new civilization, the Arioto had divided up into at least ten distinct communities, but without any true tribal organization. They respected a form of chief, chosen by tacit consent for his personal qualities rather than by name or by birth-right; but the chiefs acted merely as paternal advisers, to be respected in times of trouble, with no illusions of authority. No one commanded, and none obeyed: all were content to follow the whim of the moment, with no conception of social obligation.

When the foreigners arrived, there were five main groups of Arioto on North Andaman, the Cari, Chede, Cora, Jeru and Tabo. Another five groups were in South Andaman, the Balawa, Bea, Bogig-iab, Joi and Col. With the numerical decline of the Arioto, who had always been endogamous within their group, a tendency arose for the survivors to merge and inter-marry, so that the twenty-three alive today are in fact the result of the mixing of the northern and southern Arioto, and of these with Indians and Burmese. The chief of these twenty-three individuals is Loca, a name in itself an indication of this ethnic mixture. Loca means 'whiskers', and he himself has a moustache, whereas pure Negritos have no body or facial hair.

THE JARAWAS

For obvious reasons I was unable to carry out any studies on the Jarawas. Apart from a restricted area around Port Blair, on the east coast of Great Andaman, the whole island is a tangle of tropical vegetation, in many places impenetrable, or at most passable only by hacking a way through. A few roads radiate from Port Blair, but none penetrate more than twenty kilometres or so from the township. To the north of the town is a well-maintained police cordon that stretches right across the island from east to west to prevent infiltration by the Jarawas; those in the south were all rounded up some time ago. Only beyond the cordon do the Jarawas maintain their rule over the virgin forest almost unchallenged. Like all the Andamanese they are Negritos, small in stature and extremely dark skinned. Obsessed by a fierce hatred for anyone outside their own group, enemies even of the other Andamanese, they roam through the forest with their deadly arrows. Shot from their powerful bows, their dagger-sharp arrows penetrate deep into the body of the victim – they can transfix a man's chest. The bloody skirmishing which has gone on for the last hundred years shows no signs of lessening even today.

The Jarawa ferocity increased as the result of grave mishandling of the situation by the foreigners. In this connection the following sentences from Portman's *History* may be quoted: 'On our arrival the Jarawas were quiet and inoffensive towards us, nor did they ever disturb us, until we took to continuously molesting them by inciting the coastal Andamanese against them. After a few years of this disturbance, the life of the Jarawas became very hard and in retaliation they began to attack us.' As the author in part recognizes, 'It was our fault if the Jarawas became hostile'. This was a fundamental error. Petty pilfering committed in perfect innocence by the Jarawas, ignorant of Western ideas of individual property, led to vicious punitive expeditions. To this end fire-arms were given to the hereditary enemies of the Jarawas, the Arioto. Elated by their unexpected power, they at once began slaughtering any Jarawa within sight, and enjoyed themselves hugely.

6

Portman, who was for a long time the English administrator in the Andamans, is one of the greatest authorities on the islands; in his excellent history he refers, with frank sincerity and detail, to the methods adopted in the anti-Jarawa wars. He tells of the payment of the Arioto with food, tobacco and alcohol, arms and ammunition for their ruthless fight against their forest kin. Since at one time the struggle seemed to the outsiders to be lacking in ardour and intensity, Portman received an order in 1884 to deprive the Arioto of all provisions, starting with food. This he was forced to obey, perhaps unwillingly. He certainly loved the Andamanese, and he understood and honestly appreciated their needs.

As he later did on Little Andaman, Portman then tried to approach the Jarawas; not on Great Andaman where they had become too dangerous, but on North Sentinel. He proposed to improve upon the work already initiated (with disastrous results) by Homfray who went to the island in March 1867, escorted by police and by a small group of Arioto. The hostility between Andamanese from different localities immediately made even the Sentinelese keenly resentful of the foreigners who were trying to make friends with them under the protection of their age-old enemies. The foreigners would in fact probably have been quite well received if they had not taken Arioto with them.

Homfray referred to naked men on the beach who fled with loud cries into the forest when pursued by Arioto. Portman repeated the same mistake. In his photographs, still to be seen in the Indian Museum at Calcutta, he actually uses the expression 'Hunting Jarawas' among the captions to the pictures he took on North Sentinel.

After several abortive expeditions by Portman, visits to North Sentinel were very few and far between until recent years. In 1926 a German, whose name became anglicized to Bonington, an intelligent timber merchant at Port Blair, became a government official in the Andamans once he had assumed British nationality. He reports having seen some Jarawas, who rapidly disappeared into the forest uttering such wild cries that they hardly seemed human. In 1953 other Indian government officials approached the island, and a lone Jarawa on the beach threatened them with an arrow. I myself planned to make a landing on 20 April 1954, but was prevented by a rough sea. I went right round the island, but no Jarawas appeared.

7

This was a pity, as I knew that my Indian and Burmese companions were ready to run any risk with the prudence they had already shown in Little Andaman towards the Onges. Since North Sentinel is flat and its forest not impassable, a peace mission led by men accustomed to dealing with people like the Andamanese, though it would certainly need more than a brief stay, would probably be ultimately successful.

My sole source of local information on the Jarawas was the wife of a government official, who had tended a pregnant woman and four children who were captured during one of the punitive expeditions on Bluff Island. She gave me a great deal of useful information, and indeed the greater part of our scanty ethnographical and linguistic data on the Jarawas has been obtained through her.

THE ONGES

Until 1952 the attitude of the various groups of Onges was very similar. Along the coast, however, they had already had some contact many years ago with a limited number of outsiders. Compared with the Jarawas they have been uniquely fortunate among surviving primitive peoples in that their extremely fertile territory has remained immune from invasion. In this they have been helped by their geographical isolation as much as by their own ferocity. Indeed Little Andaman, surrounded by an ocean that frequently turns into the proverbial boiling cauldron, presents grave risks to anyone trying to land. I had considerable experience of this myself; on many occasions I nearly gave up when the boat was overturned by giant breakers. On one occasion on the south coast of the island we were flung into the sea, and the empty boat capsized and dragged me down. No one was in a position to come to my rescue, but the momentary relief of an enormous return wave enabled me to extricate myself. The previous day the breakers had crashed down one after another and smashed us against the coral reef which runs right round Little Andaman. Our baggage and provisions had disappeared, and until help arrived we were forced to remain for two gruelling days without water or food, with no protection from the sun and in constant danger of being attacked by the Onges.

During the course of the nineteenth and twentieth centuries

there have been many attempts by outsiders to land on Little Andaman, but until recently none have gone beyond the coast, and the interior of the island remained unknown until 1952. Several people were drowned in the tremendous breakers, and a few were killed by the aboriginals. The last (undocumented) incident, involving Chinese sailors in search of water on the west coast of the island, appears to have taken place in 1949. There are no records of any attempt to land before 1825, when an English naval officer, T. E. Alexander, managed to do so, and was the first to report, in England, the existence of a fierce tribe of naked Onges. The encounter was bloody, as were many afterwards. Rumours (erroneous) were spread of cannibalism, as some English sailors who had managed to save themselves saw their companions being torn to pieces by the Onges: their hands, feet, legs and arms were cut off and the living remains were thrown into a great fire. This was, in fact, not cannibalism, but the satisfying of a superstition, already recorded by various well-known authorities on the Andamans, such as Portman, Radcliffe-Brown and others, that the spirit is immortal and stays by its bones. The spirit of an enemy could thus become a disturbing influence, which is to be avoided by totally destroying the living body with fire, so that the spirit flies with the smoke towards the sky, where it remains.

Some time after Alexander, various English officials tempted providence in Little Andaman[1] and finally, on 24 July 1885, Portman landed, and began intensive efforts to pacify the Onges. Well protected by a police force, he was the first man who had the courage to pitch camp on the coast of Little Andaman. For most of March 1886, he stayed in the north of the island, and then between 28 October 1886 and 21 January 1887, he went slowly right round the island, starting from his camp at Bumila Creek. In the same year, two officials of the Indian Cartographic Service sailed round the entire coastline of Little Andaman; the resulting survey was, however, very imperfect. Portman returned for a brief visit to Bumila Creek in March 1887. This time there was a serious incident with the Onges, culminating in the severe wounding of an English

[1] Homfray, 1867; Stewart, 1873; Homfray and Stewart, 1874; Cadel, 1880; Cadel and Portman, 1880; Portman, 1880 and 1882; Man, 1883; various abortive landings, 1884 and 1885.

colonel who had accompanied him. After a series of similar incidents involving other people Portman went to Bumila Creek on 10 November 1891, for revenge. A number of Onges, including the one responsible for wounding the colonel, were captured and taken to Port Blair.

Other visits by various people followed, always very brief and always limited to the coast, but there were no landings of note. Various expeditions visited the coast of the island for a few days and even made contact with some of the Onges, but the interior of the island remained as unknown as before. In February 1951 I accompanied one of these expeditions, which again did not go beyond the coast. Those five days on Little Andaman were most revealing, and enabled me to plan the landing I subsequently made in 1952. I saw that the island was teeming with game, that wild fruit and edible roots were plentiful, and that the sea round the island was full of fish, lobsters, huge crabs and turtles. Moreover, the turtles laid eggs in the sand where it was very easy to find them by following the beasts' tracks. I realized that it would be unnecessary to bring in provisions, and that it would be possible to enter the forest unencumbered with anything more than guns, cartridges and a few cooking utensils. Every day during this short stay I went with a police escort as far as possible into the forest in order to reconnoitre. In some places I noticed recent traces of small bare feet, but no Onges appeared.

Realizing that mobility was essential for any expedition into the interior of the island, I prepared at Port Blair a number of small watertight metal boxes to hang from the shoulder, to take a minimum of necessities. The largest items in my own personal baggage were a mosquito-net, a very light hammock and note-books. Cartridges were to be divided among the boxes. Tents, camp-beds and other large equipment would have to be left in a base camp, which would be established on the coast and left under police guard with radio transmission apparatus for communication with Port Blair. If necessary, a portable radio could follow us.

Several factors made me want to return. There was the mystery of the unknown interior of the island. There was the prevailing lack of information of any kind about the Onges, even of their numbers. I wanted too to carry out an investigation of their somatic characteristics, using the greatest possible number of individuals.

After submitting my programme for the approval of the various Indian authorities, I finally left Calcutta in the motor vessel *Maharaja* and arrived in Port Blair on the evening of 11 December 1951.

Once arrived on Great Andaman I began to make preparations, but for some time the sea remained so rough that the crossing to Little Andaman was impossible. In order not to lose time, I went as far as Middle Andaman, where I started excavating an ancient kitchen-midden left by a group which has now disappeared.[1] Eventually, in March 1952, there began for me what was to become a fascinating if dangerous adventure, which continued for several years, in the dry seasons, and which I hope will prove to have been of some value.

Even now we know little of the anthropology of the Onges. They are Negritos, and therefore people of small stature. They are not, however, as small as the African pygmies, or Negrillos, who are the tiniest people in the world and who are in many respects very different from the Asiatic Negritos. Among the latter, individuals of over 4 feet are giants, while the normal height is substantially less.

In their somatic and cultural characteristics the Andamanese differ from all Asiatics, including their closest connections the Semang of the Malaccan peninsula and the Aetà of the Philippines. There is however some similarity between the three groups, indicating a distinctive common ancestry. The Negritos of today constitute the sole and fragmentary remains of a people who in ancient times were spread over a large part of Asia, and there is no lack of evidence to support their former presence much farther east and south, well into Oceania.

The word Negrito means 'small negro', but the name is inappropriate. It was originally given to these people because of the colour of their skin and the woolly texture of their hair. In their bodily proportions, however, as well as in the morphology of the head as a whole, and in particular the structure of the mouth, they resemble the Negroes considerably less than do African pygmies, who are in their turn quite a distinct type. The Negritos have some superficial affinity to peoples of small stature in New Guinea and Melanesia, such as the Tapiro, the Cameveca, the Cai and the Pesechem (or

[1] See page 69.

Pesekem), although they are distinguished from them by profound cultural differences. These differences exist even between the three groups of Negritos. Whereas in Malacca and the Philippines they reflect the influx of superior cultures, these have had very little influence in the Andamans. For this reason the Andamanese have perforce remained more faithful to very ancient customs, and are also somatically the least altered.

The study of the last remaining groups, the Onges and Jarawas, now on the point of extinction if they are not protected, is thus a matter of singular urgency and significance.

We know nothing of how the Negritos arrived in their present homes with somatic and cultural characteristics quite distinct from those of any other human type. Apart from some dubious remains excavated in Indochina we do not even have any fossil remains to show their probable original distribution. There is, however, reason to believe that they were once very widely dispersed, judging from the evidence of their presence today as isolates widely separated from each other.

No traces of them remain in the continental areas adjacent to the Andamans, apart from the Malaccan peninsula. At one time it was thought that traces of a Negrito element were to be found in the Kadir of Hindustan, revealed by the occasional presence of curly hair. I have myself visited the area, and must refute this suggestion; the people have nothing of the Negrito in their body structure, their hair is markedly longer than the Negrito and they have body hair. The kinky hair (never woolly) occasionally seen may derive from distant Negro crosses, or may be an accidental similarity. I have seen this type of curliness even in Europeans who certainly had no Negro or pygmy ancestry.

It has also been asserted, possibly with some foundation, although there are few data available, that there are traces of the Negrito among the people of New Guinea, such as the Tapiro. Although of small stature, their general characteristics would seem to relate the Tapiro more closely to the Papuans; they have yellowish skin, probably the lightest in that area, they are, again, hirsute and there is a marked absence of Negrito characteristics in the proportions of the body.

The first thing that strikes one on meeting the Onges – and indeed the Andamanese in general – is the exceptional blackness and softness of their skin. They have what must be among the darkest skins in the world, and in certain lights some individuals have a bluish tinge, which I have never seen in any other region. Something similar seems to have existed among the now extinct Tasmans, although they differed markedly from the Andamanese in other respects. The Onges are the only Andamanese who are not invariably intensely black, and the bluish type is rare among them. This might be attributable to contact with the nearby Nicobars, where a yellowish skin is common, in conjunction with Mongoloid features. I saw no traces, however, of such admixture; the Arioto show some sign of recent Burmese influence, but any ethnic influences on the Onges and Jarawas must have been extremely ancient, indeed before their arrival in the archipelago. In the south and south-west of Little Andaman I did find individuals markedly taller than the rest (though still small), but it is clear that outwardly at least the Onges and Jarawas still retain most of their unique somatic characteristics, which have remained unchanged for thousands of years.

The Andamanese skin is very smooth in texture, and lacks the odour characteristic of many of the African peoples. This would appear to depend on the chemical composition of the sweat, as the Andamanese never intentionally wash, although brushing against the sodden vegetation, and frequent immersion while collecting shellfish, or fishing, in some measure compensates. Curiously enough their sweat does seem to repel the local ticks, which drive Europeans mad; again, it was interesting that the Indians and Burmese of my party were variously affected by them.

Their skin is also extraordinarily elastic – I noticed that in the forest I scratched myself continually at the slightest touch against thorns or branches, whereas the Onges invariably emerged quite unscathed at the end of the trek. Their greater agility of movement will undoubtedly have been part of the answer, but it would be impossible to avoid any scratches, as they do, unless their skin 'gave' to an abnormal degree.

Another effect of this elasticity is that the women suffer no disfiguration of the skin over the abdomen after childbirth, and neither sex becomes wrinkled to any noticeable extent with age. This distinguishes them clearly from peoples with whom they have been compared – such as the Bushmen, who (possibly in part due to the arid climate) are among the most wrinkled people in the world.

At birth, the Onges are tiny, attractive little creatures, very plump, but rarely over two and a half kilograms in males and two kilograms in females. I was very fortunate indeed in that I succeeded in persuading one young couple to let me examine their new-born child. Local superstition forbids a stranger looking on a child for any length of time, and even an Onge who does so is regarded with suspicion, so I had to be extremely cautious.

The infant was born on 30 March 1954, in the forest to the north of Labanar. Like most deliveries, birth took place in the forest on a bed improvised for the purpose, with only the father (on some occasions also the wife's mother) present, and the placenta was buried under the bed. The women recover very quickly;[1] after a few days they are fit for heavy work, returning to the group without any purification ceremonies, and this was no exception. After a wealth of gifts I managed to examine the child on the morning of 31 March and again on 10, 13 and 14 April. After this mother and child vanished completely, and the father would give me only evasive replies, although only a few days before he had been willing to help me open some graves round Tambe-e-buiè, allowing me to remove the bones of nine Onges who had been dead for many years; superstition (or the women) overcame him on this occasion, however.

My examinations were all carried out in the presence of the mother and at least two of the older women, who were determined to prevent me touching the child.

The child, like all Onge babies, had no body hair; this persists throughout life, though some males have sparse moustaches. Its head was covered with a very fine, sparse down, not black like the adults, but already showing signs of the characteristic woolly texture. Dark reddish-brown, the hair becomes black and tightly curled during the first year of life. The eyelashes curl markedly in adults, but the hair of the eyebrows is virtually straight; in the infant the former were barely visible, and the latter completely absent.

The nails were strong and well formed, projecting a little beyond

[1] Childbirth is normally very easy, but miscarriages are common, probably due to lack of vitality in the foetus.

the finger-tips and almost pink, with pale chocolate moons and yellowish-brown palms and soles. In the adults the nails and soles of the feet remain pale, the palms being a little darker. The head, and the visible buccal and nasal epithelia, were almost black, and the gums were pink, as was the inside of the lips, with dark petecchiae, in adults very noticeable, at the base of the teeth and over the tongue and palate. The cheeks, however, were a reddish-brown, although the whole skin was already showing signs of darkening after twelve hours. Nasal cartilage was minimal, but that of the ears well-developed. The darkest area of skin were the forehead, eye sockets, lids, nipples and genitalia.

In general, therefore, the infant's skin was very slightly lighter than that of the adults, though before I could be sure of this I had to wash off the thick layer of ochre which is smeared over the unwashed infants immediately after birth. As the infants are extremely carefully protected from the sun by 'umbrella' hats made of lobed palm leaves, the darkening, which is complete by the end of the first year, is clearly biological and is not effected by tanning. As, however, the Onges interchange or 'adopt' children freely, it was impossible to carry out any proper colorimetric observations.

I saw no albinos in the Onges, usually fairly common in dark-skinned peoples. I saw several in Africa, with apparently normal parents. Some African peoples destroy albinos at birth as they do those with deformities, and the Andamanese may do the same, as I saw little congenital deformity (see, however, p. 46). Fear of being held responsible for disasters which befall the group carries great weight, and it is possible that the two cases of abnormality which I did see did not manifest symptoms at birth. Twins, however, are clearly (and gladly) accepted, so eager are the Onges to have children.

It was already clear in the infant that it would have the somatic characteristics common to all Negritos as regards the proportions of the body, the form and dimensions of the head, absence of prognathism, comparatively fine lips, nose and ears, black skin, and woolly hair, and would be well below 1·5 metres in height when fully grown. Above all, the Andamanese have a large forehead, very wide-angled jaw and large mouths, with the upper lips not invariably full, as in Negroes. Many Onges, in fact, have fine features,

and some of the women have a certain beauty and grace of movement, with a dignified walk and restrained gestures, despite their
utter lack of any sense of shame. The sclera are very white, and the
highly characteristic contrast between the intense black of the skin
and the startling white of the eyes gives the Andamanese a ferocious
appearance, which on smiling turns into a curiously childish expression (see further, p. 19). It is a curious fact that although the
Onges have remarkable sight (p. 47), few of them can close each
eye separately, although they are all completely ambidextrous.

In examining the child I had particularly in mind the very short
stature of the pygmies both of Asia and Africa, which is regarded
by some as pathological. The Andamanese have been described as
Negroes who have degenerated through genetical isolation. This
theory holds that they are descended from slaves who fled from the
Portuguese after a shipwreck. I do not regard this as tenable.
Pygmies in general, and the Andamanese in particular, are well-
proportioned and physically outwardly normal. One cannot speak
of dwarfism as determining their characteristics: this implies abnormal development as the result of hypophyseal disorder or
thyroid imbalance. Cases of achondroplastic dwarfism are known
among the pygmies of Africa, particularly where there has been
mixing with Negroes, and these patients are sometimes taller than
their normal kinfolk, but I found no cases among the pygmies of
Asia.

One characteristic of the Bushmen which does occur among the
Andamanese is steatopigia in both males and females. This is normally much more prevalent in females, and indeed before my visit
to the Andamans von Eickstedt held that it was non-existent in
males. I had always disagreed with this view, and was able to verify
its occurrence in both males and females.

Dobson in the nineteenth century recorded in the *Journal of the
Royal Anthropological Institute* of London, the unusual appearance of
the buttocks in the Andamanese, although he did not specifically
refer to the phenomenon as steatopygia, and went only so far as to
suppose it the result of an unusual accumulation of fat in the gluteal
area. To him, however, must go the credit for the first observation.

His observation led scientists – in my view wrongly – to compare
the Andamanese with the Bushmen. The presence of steatopygia,

and the 'peppercorn' hair (disposed in tufts with bare areas) do indeed recall the Bushmen, but superficial resemblances are not enough to classify the two peoples as at all closely related. There is an important difference between the two in the structure and cross-section of the hair. Hairs from the Onges which were examined in Calcutta were remarkably uniform, indicating the racial purity of the people, unlike those of the Arioto, which showed considerable variation in cross-section, from the almost circular straight hair of the Mongoloid type, to the flattened, almost remiform hair of the original Negritos.

Different, too, is the shape of the head; I have never seen in the Negritos the typical Bushmen head, with the prominent occiput, and I saw no Andamanese with the pseudo-mongoloid appearance of the eyes which occurs in Bushmen.

The hands and feet are also different. Among the Kung women of the northern Kalahari in particular I saw delicate hands with very long metacarpals and a very small thumb, the elongated metacarpals displacing the thumb towards the wrist. None of the Negritos appear to have anything resembling this; their hands are always rather broad. Moreover, the feet of the male Onges are nearly always flat while those of the women tend to turn in, recalling the small peoples of Indonesia and New Guinea, but not the Bushmen.

An interesting though not congenital abnormality in the Andamanese results from the carrying of weights slung from the head from too early an age. Loads are always carried on their backs by a rope made of bark, the weight being taken on the forehead. The rope presses on the head in the region of the bregma and creates the so-called bregmatic furrow. This is more marked in females, as the women normally do most of the carrying. Even the children travel on their parents' backs, hanging like parcels, until the age of five or six when they are old enough to follow the group on their own.

The Abor, a mongoloid people of small stature in the mountains of North-West Assam, carry loads in the same way, but with no resulting head furrow. The Andamanese have softer cranial bones, and the result of load-bearing is therefore clearly visible. As it occurs in both sexes, it is often hard if not impossible to determine sex from skulls if the pelvis is absent. The long bones are not of much assistance in this respect, as the muscular insertions are exaggerated in both sexes, both being subjected to continued physical effort resulting in muscular bulk.

One quite outstanding physical feature in the Onges is their teeth. The palate is unusually arched, unlike that of the African pygmies or the Bushmen. The teeth, which are never filed or cut, as many primitive peoples do for decorative purposes, are very white; caries is rare, and although never cleaned the teeth are retained till late in life. A common abnormality is that the lateral incisors are as pointed as the canines. This, with the whiteness of the teeth and eyes against the blackness of the skin, gives the Onges a sinister appearance, which may account for the old description of the Andamanese as men with ferocious dogs' heads. The only (summary) cleaning the Onge teeth receive is the use of toothpicks, thinner and rather longer than the European variety and made from the tough, flexible bark of a certain reed. After use, they are carefully thrust into the hair for future occasions. Every Onge has one or more threaded through the hair on top of the head.

The strength of the Onge teeth enables their owners to champ their way through what are for us inconceivable quantities of food, both animal and vegetable, which is chewed slowly and determinedly, dust, earth, sand and all, and then swallowed without apparent ill effects, other than the flatulence arising from overconsumption of animal matter. But the Onges use their teeth for other purposes besides eating. In time the teeth become worn down by the inevitable grinding of dirt and grit, but this does not prevent the Onges from continuing to chew the bark of trees and cords, which is a lifelong occupation. This duty falls mainly on the women, and I have seen aged women, their teeth worn almost to the gums, doggedly chewing bark as their contribution to the communal life of the group. The strength of the teeth is unbelievable – I have seen children of ten to fifteen years crush nails up to two millimetres thick, and dent lumps of iron.

I myself once had good cause to be grateful for their power. My party and I found ourselves stranded in the forest on South Brother without guns or even knives, and without cooking utensils. There were large clutches of turtle eggs buried in the sand nearby and my two Onge companions pointed out a coconut tree loaded with nuts (which turned out to be the only one on the islands, seeded from a nut carried by the sea from some tree hundreds of miles away). There was thus ample food for several days, if only the coconuts could be opened. The Onges' teeth solved the problem. They attacked the nuts close to the stalk, stripping off great chunks of the fibrous outer covering until they had uncovered the three 'eyes'. These they dug out with a sharp piece of stick, so that we were able to drink the juice and then break up the nuts to get at the flesh. Never did coconuts taste so good!

Round the base of the tree I saw a thick layer of broken pieces of coconut, the remains of nuts opened by the Onges' teeth over the years. The strength of their bite resembles that of the African pygmies, whom I have seen hanging by their teeth from the lianas and who can dent the barrel of a gun.

The average life span of the Onges, and indeed of the Andamanese in general, is fairly short. On Little Andaman there are probably no individuals over the age of sixty, and most die before fifty. Here again they differ from African peoples of similar stature; Bushmen have been known to live to a hundred, and I saw one in Natal, incredibly wrinkled, but not shrunken, who was certainly near that age if not, as he claimed, over it. This is quite unknown in the Andamanese. There are none with white hair; although a few white hairs can sometimes be found on the head of an old woman, there are none to be seen in the men, who die younger than the women. There is no baldness, which is by no means rare in Negroes, particularly in southern Africa.

Precise age is not easy to determine in the Onges. Visual assessment is hampered by the absence of the signs of ageing common in Europeans. Moreover, a particularly child-like expression often lasts into adult life. In May 1952 I saw on Car Nicobar two Jarawa youths, small but robust, whose age by our standards one would have estimated at ten or twelve years. One turned out to be fourteen, however, and the other at least two years older, and both were adolescent, despite their childish appearance.

Males appear to reach their maximum height at about eighteen, and females at about sixteen; both sexes reach full maturity at about twenty-three. At forty-five they are old: their hard life, their unbalanced diet, with its enormous quantities of fat meat eaten in excess, and complete absence of salt, and their unrestrained sexual activity, may all be contributing factors. The slightly greater age

reached by the women may possibly be explained by their somewhat less arduous life physically, but biological factors may be the
root cause. Despite their deceptively youthful appearance the
menopause is over by the age of thirty-eight, at the latest, and they
remain in good health thereafter, looking amazingly young. The
oldest man I saw was Enagaghe, the head of one of the groups, and
he could not have been more than fifty-five. He happily accompanied me on long and arduous trips into the forest, and climbed
trees like a squirrel after honey and fruit; neither his appetite nor
his zeal as a lover were impaired. His stomach managed to cope
with something like a kilo a day of meat, skin and fat, plus fruit,
boiled roots and honey. In a hot, damp, oppressive climate like
that of the Andamans such a diet year after year cannot fail to
produce a state of chronic intestinal poisoning likely to affect the
organism as a whole, and may contribute to shorten life, despite
an apparent physical vigour.

Connected, perhaps, with their excesses is the fact that the Onges'
normal body temperature is much higher than usual; with a temperature reading of thirty-eight degrees centigrade they are in good
health, with unimpaired appetite. I found an average temperature
of thirty-seven point five degrees centigrade in males of various
ages, the younger men tending to give the higher readings. The
average in females was slightly higher than in males. I was able to
observe for myself completely normal behaviour in Onges who by
European standards would have been regarded as severely febrile.
In part, as I have said, this may be due to diet and absence of salt,
but it must certainly be regarded at least in part as a racial characteristic. It may, too, have some effect on their low vitality; it is
interesting that temperatures in the Bushmen and pygmies of
Africa, with their longer expectation of life, never vary far from
the European norm.

These abnormally high temperatures are not a symptom of
malaria. This is clinically unknown in the Andamanese although it
is a serious menace to outsiders. Even a few hours on the island can
lead to infection if precautions are not taken. I made all the men
with me take their tablets regularly, even when propaganda in
India against immunization as a Western importation led to objec-
tions, so that I had to force the tablets into their mouths myself to
ensure that they were swallowed.

The Onges do not seem to require any preventive measures, and seem naturally immune to malaria. They do, however, transmit the disease to strangers, through the mosquitoes which are everywhere in Little Andaman. Like many other inhabitants of tropical areas, they probably all carry the disease without being affected by it – neither children nor adults show any sign of splenic enlargement.

In contrast to their periodic gorging, the Onges will equally cheerfully endure hunger, thirst and exhaustion. During our hazardous canoe trip to South Brother, however, they appeared much more affected than I was by long exposure to the sun. We were completely without any means of shelter for an entire afternoon in the open sea, and though the Onges tried to cover their heads as best they could, they still developed severe (and genuine) headaches, and were clearly much happier in the dark forest, which must be considered their natural environment.

Nothing has hitherto been known of the intelligence level and general psychology of the Onges. The childishness of their behaviour, however, is curiously in keeping with their strikingly child-like appearance. Like children, they seek only the satisfaction of elementary stimuli, and like children they pass in a flash from one mood to another, so that they are a people of sudden contrasts.

One example is their passionate love for their dogs, in marked contrast to the intense cruelty with which they hunt their prey. Having once realized the usefulness of dogs, first imported into the islands some thirty years ago, the Onges now pet them like little girls with their dolls, and the Onge women will suckle the family puppies quite naturally with their own children. Yet once a dog dies the other side of the Onge nature comes to the fore and the carcase is thrown into the forest – there is no looking back.

Their minds are in a sense inventive, in that they have evolved devices to help them acquire their food, but they have never, for example, thought of the fish-hook, despite the abundance of iron pieces thrown up by shipwrecks all round the islands. Anything new is taken up with a child's momentary enthusiasm, but they have no notion of sustained mental effort such as any form of counting.

Like children, too, the Onges laugh at the slightest thing, although their mirth is always restrained. In this they differ from the African peoples, particularly the Bushmen, who are often by

Western standards taciturn or sly, and the Negro peoples, who frequently manifest complete abandonment in their amusement. Obscenities appear to be an unfailing source of amusement to the Onges, who indulge in them at every opportunity, even with strangers, and the obscene dances of the womenfolk are a continual source of pleasure. The exchange of obscenities is, indeed, a sign of friendship, and I found that vulgarity was invariably immensely successful in provoking hilarity; any subsequent negotiations were always peaceable and satisfactory.

An extension of this vulgarity is an infantile vanity, not without sexual significance. The care with which their bodies are painted nearly every day is one aspect of this vanity; the more a wife loves her husband the more magnificent the designs she executes on him. The paintings on their bodies reach a peak every two or three days, as the Onges fear illness and death if they are not newly daubed, and the face at least must be continually painted, with at least smears on the chest, arms and legs. A man returning from an exceptionally successful hunting trip is met by his wife with a specially unusual and elaborate design, which she carries out with great devotion. During each of my visits to the island the Onges would rush up to show me their embellishments as soon as they were finished, and took a delight in standing in front of my camera, even though they had no idea what it was for.

It is curious that unlike most primitive peoples, the Onges do not practise tattooing, which is one of the simplest ways, if not *the* simplest, in which such peoples satisfy their craving for physical admiration. The other Andamanese do, puncturing the skin with tiny slivers of obsidian or quartz, but the Onges paint with ochre instead. They love, too, to weave garlands of fruit, flowers and leaves from the forest, returning to the camp laden with them, men and women alike, delighted with their own beauty. This divergence of customs in peoples essentially of the same stock, but separated for long periods of time into endogamous isolates, is very remarkable.

An intense preoccupation with sexual attraction and activity has led to the prevalence of aberration. All the Onges have homosexual tendencies. I became aware of this during my first visit to Little Andaman on one of my longer expeditions, when I had taken only men with me, and on subsequent occasions I therefore allowed the men to bring their wives. The effect of long periods of absence on men naturally predisposed to the abnormality is enhanced by the fact that the youngest and most attractive women are invariably monopolized by the older men. So prevalent, indeed, is homo-sexuality that one is obliged to regard it as a biological, and not as a social or psychological abnormality. It is not, therefore, surprising to find that kissing is unknown; sexual excitement is aroused instead by nose-rubbing.

None of the Onges have any sense of modesty. This is partly the result of circumstances; privacy is impossible in the communal life of the group. This is in marked contrast to the comical dignity assumed during the last few years by the remaining Arioto women. The government authorities decreed that they should be clothed, and they immediately became so prudish that they refuse to bare so much as an arm, and they thus present a considerable problem to the anthropologist. Their menfolk, however, are clearly de-lighted with this sudden modesty which was to me a somewhat pathetic parody, and a further example of Andamanese childish-

CHAPTER TWO

The Silent Forest

The whole of the Andamans and Nicobars can be regarded as the top of an oceanic mountain range, an extension of the Arakan mountains of Burma, which continues out under the sea from Cape Nigrais. Geological structure and flora are very similar, although there are some significant differences in the fauna, due to the subsequent isolation of the archipelago.

On Great Andaman there are many rocks of continental origin, but they are rare on Little Andaman, where the surface largely consists of coral deposits on top of sedimentary and volcanic rocks. At some points on the east coast the sea throws up lumps of fine, very hard granite; I found an outcrop of it in Butler Bay, to the north of Hut Bay, and another at Labanar near the river Tejàh. In the central area are some hills of sedimentary rock all less than a hundred metres high, dropping towards the south of the island. The whole of the rest of the island is built up of coral deposit.

Various geological events, still in progress, caused the separation of Great and Little Andaman. The former, three hundred and twenty kilometres north to south, suffered in the course of time two transverse fractures east to west, large enough for fair-sized steamers to pass through. The rift is so narrow that in places one can throw a stone across. These two marine channels, as we have seen, divided Great Andaman into the Islands now known as North, Middle and South Andaman.

The Andamans are still subject to frequent earthquakes, often quite strong ones, which are gradually altering the conformation of the islands just as long ago they divided Great Andaman. From my excavations in the kitchen-middens I was able to verify changes in the level of marine life, due not to any variation in the level of the sea itself, but to the rising and falling of the land with the recurring movements. Even between 1951 and 1952 there was a noticeable alteration in the level of the north-east coast of Little Andaman, following an earthquake in July 1951; the Onges had to move the communal hut at Tambe-e-buiè further inland, because the sea, previously twenty metres away, had begun to come right up to the hut. In several places giant trees centuries old crashed to the ground, their roots left without any foothold as the level of the land fell suddenly all along the coast. If this can happen in one year, it is hardly surprising that what now appears as an archipelago is in reality a continuous mountain chain, its levels broken and rebroken over thousands of years till the islands became separated by the sea for good, their coasts so eroded that subsequent quakes have failed to reunite them.

It is highly unwise even to attempt a landing on Little Andaman during the monsoons. Both the north-east monsoon in June and August and the south-west in November and January whip the seas up into a frenzy, but in late April and again in late September the sea is quite calm. Since both monsoons pass over vast tracts of sea, they become saturated with water vapour and bring torrential rains, not infrequently accompanied by hurricanes violent enough to strip all the leaves off the trees. After these storms the jungle, normally almost impenetrable, is made even more so by the tangle of fallen branches and the trunks of old trees torn up by the wind or the lightning. The lightning strikes the tallest trees, which may smoulder for days on end without setting fire to the sodden forest, so great is the humidity. I have often seen one of these flaming torches; the Onges, ignorant as they are of the art of making fire, take advantage of the phenomenon, as a continuous supply of burning wood is a necessity in a climate which is so damp and humid all the year round that matches become useless after twenty-four hours unless suitable precautions are taken.

Once on the island, virgin forest stretches endlessly before one in undulating waves of treetops, black and terrifying. From the tops of the trees thousands of lianas hang everywhere, winding like snakes from trunk to trunk, forming an inextricable tangle, yet somehow always elegant, binding the entire forest into one dense mass. Many of the tree-trunks reach diameters unheard of in temperate climates. Some of them have hollow cavities, treasured by the Onges as hiding-places or temporary shelters. In these cavities, which remain full of water right through the dry season, flourish a horde of amphibia, many hitherto unknown.

The great trees are sometimes so close together that it is literally impossible to pass between them, yet it is rare to find two of the same species next to each other, so great is the variety. Huge clumps of ferns are everywhere, hiding the roots of dying trees, hundreds of years old, and fallen trunks rotting on the ground. Some of the thicker and taller trees protect themselves from the monsoon gales by developing buttresses, usually four or six to a tree, which stand out from the trunk like right-angled triangles, with the apex about ten metres from the ground. If a blanket is stretched between the sloping sides of two of the buttresses one can improvise a shelter which is extremely comfortable by local standards, and both man and animals take advantage of this natural cover; I myself took shelter like this on many occasions. (They need to be treated with caution, however, as the local snakes have a predilection for siestas in the darkest corners.) If a hard piece of wood is struck against one of the buttresses it echoes hollowly, and the Andamanese often make use of them to transmit warning messages over considerable distances, using a form of code. A few beats can make every inhabitant within a wide radius vanish from sight, hastily making for the nearest hiding-place. It is hopeless to try and ferret them out once they have been warned, and there is always a risk of being killed by one of their arrows in the process.

Sometimes the Onges used to disappear suddenly for fun. The blackness of their skin is a great help in this, since even on the brightest afternoon it is intensified by the obscurity of the forest. One has a disturbing sensation of being entirely alone, yet knowing that dozens of pairs of eyes are watching as the Onges glide silently from trunk to trunk between the buttresses.

The whole island is a mass of knotted vegetation, and it is useless to attempt to cut any form of lasting path, as the plants immediately grow back. 'Walking' in the Andamans therefore means opening up a way with a hatchet, unless one adopts the rapid but exhausting Onge method of swinging over obstacles by the lianas. This is the kingdom of the epiphytes. The lianas cover their hosts as if determined to hide them, and clumps of orchids hang from nearly every trunk, although their flowers are unfortunately very small.

It is impossible to imagine a more varied or richer sight than the Andamanese forests at any time of year. The colours, and the light effects, particularly at dawn and at sunset, the myriads of flowers of every hue and scent, every shape and size, the strange noises, all combine to produce an effect which stuns the outsider. The spectacle reaches its climax at night when the moon is full; the tops of the trees are bathed in a silver light and the great lianas seem to writhe like serpents. As though inspired by the light, the nocturnal animals stage a kind of pageant for the occasion and their cries are even more frequent and more rhythmic than usual. The Andamanese themselves seem bewitched without realizing it, spellbound by the weird atmosphere.

To anyone unfamiliar with the tropics, the swift change from darkness to light and back again comes as a surprise. Night in the tropics is never silent – the eerie voices and calls, often with a strange pitch, seem to cease for a brief moment just before the sudden onset of darkness and again just before the return of the light. As night falls the fascination of the jungle grows. Even the natives feel some urge to keep their voices down, as if out of respect for some natural solemnity. (This, however, is not exclusive to the Andamanese, and it has a perfectly rational explanation. In tropical forests, and in the deserts, men speak softly so as to catch every slightest sound, a passing animal perhaps.) At dawn the birds start up as though they were tired of silence. There is no great variety of calls; most are very piercing, although still pleasing, and in the crescendo of sound which follows the dusk and dawn silences, the forest is transformed.

One thing that has helped the Onges to survive so long despite the inevitability of their decline is the climate of the islands, which is usually very pleasant and so less liable to exacerbate biological weaknesses.

Normally, the Andamans have four months of very good weather from December to March, which may extend by a few days into November and April. February is nearly always the driest month and the calmest, although there are exceptions, as I know from my own experiences when trying to land on the island. In the remaining months there is frequent rain, sometimes torrential, with raging seas, but relieved by periods of clear sky.

In the absence of rain the air is clear with few extremes of temperature, and mean temperatures are fairly constant throughout the year. Towards the end of March and throughout April, the thermometer rarely rises above twenty-five degrees centigrade in the shade, although it can rise above thirty-five degrees centigrade in the middle of the day. Heavy rains, which reduce the temperature noticeably, begin in mid-April; but a period of relatively dry, almost cold weather may occur at the beginning of May. The south-west monsoon reaches its peak in the middle of May, and continues to the end of November. During this period the temperature is never high, but the rains are frequently torrential; storms and terrific gales follow one after another and in some years the monsoons are so violent that the trees are completely stripped of their leaves in a matter of hours. Even so, there are sudden calms and in August there may be some very fine days, among the best of the year when they occur.

This climate, with its very minor variations in temperature, is explained by the geographical position of the islands. The two main islands of the archipelago run north–south, between 10° 30′ and 13° 30′ North and 90° and 92° 33′ East, rarely over forty kilometres wide. Great Andaman alone is three hundred and twenty kilometres long and Little Andaman is fifty kilometres. With the south-west monsoon the west coast faces the brunt of the storms, while the north-east monsoon hits the eastern coastline. Both hit the islands after crossing vast expanses of the Indian Ocean, but the south-west monsoon is the wetter; together they refresh the highly fertile earth.

Little Andaman forms about a sixth of this area. Its southernmost point touches 10° 30′ North and the northern tip is 10° 56′ North. On the west coast the monsoon winds are so strong and go on for so long that they have affected the growth of vegetation, beating the tops of the trees down towards the north-east, while both monsoons carry the sea spray right across the island.

With the continual dampness and relatively even temperature the forests rise before one as the coastline approaches, black, savagely beautiful, unconquered and unconquerable. Like all the rain forests of the tropics they are always a lush green, except where the monsoon has stripped the trees of their leaves. Normally the trees do not lose their leaves in the winter; each species has its own growth period, but there are so many of them that there are green leaves, and trees and plants in flower or fruit, all the year round.

There are, of course, more trees and shrubs without leaves when the heat and the dry season are at their peak, during our winter. None lose their leaves all at once, however, and in most cases they fall gradually throughout the year, accompanied by the continuous appearance of new growth. In the absence of any definite seasonal cycles, the trees grow almost continuously, so that they have no marked growth rings corresponding to the various seasons. Nor is there any sudden colouring of the leaves *en masse* with the onset of autumn; instead a permanent range of colours makes the forest incredibly beautiful at any time of the year.

Sometimes in the dry season one sees the tree known as the Flame of the Forest, one of the Leguminosae, standing out against all the others with its vermilion-red flowers, visible for considerable distances on the slopes of the hills. Rather larger than our acacia, it loses all its leaves at the beginning of January, to become covered with a mass of large flowers. I have seen similar trees in South Africa; covered with a profusion of brilliant flowers they are a wonderful sight, standing out like a sheet of flame against the sombre background of the forest round them. Even the lianas seem to respect them and leave them alone, as though fearing the slenderness of the branches, so that the trees rise like prisoners escaped by chance from the suffocating blanket of climbers all round them.

The strangling *Ficus* seems to escape them too, although lianas rage everywhere in the Andamans, their path strewn with victims. One seed of these voracious plants, left with a bird's droppings, can mean the death of a giant tree. If it lodges on a branch, or in a fork where there is a little moss or earth, it will grow and send its ropes of aerial roots down to find the earth. As soon as they touch the earth they root tenaciously, sending back energy for further growth. In a few years the ropes begin to enfold the tree, clinging to it and fusing together, till in the end there is nothing but an insidious, clinging network right round the trunk which first gave it shelter.

Every stage of this process is to be seen in the forest, from the initial unseen assault by the tiny aerial roots to the complete enveloping of the victim. Right from the first there is no escape; the

29

chance landing of a tiny seed means inevitable death by strangulation and the new plant ends by covering its victim with its own
leaves, rising above the wreck till it looks like an independent tree.

In another form this struggle between plant and plant goes on
all over the Andamans. In many places, especially where the ground
is flat, the foliage overhead kills the undergrowth by cutting off
the light. The tops of the trees, thickened by the festoons of
climbers growing over them, form a blanket high above the
ground, keeping out the light in their own struggle to reach the
sun. In the darkness below the vegetation is sparse and thin, and I
took advantage of the fact many times on journeys on Little Andaman, and also on Bluff Island, Long Island and Great Andaman.
On the steeper slopes, all thickly wooded, the sun penetrates more
easily, however, and the undergrowth flourishes, particularly
thorny plants, and the need to try and avoid being gashed always
added considerably to the effort of struggling up the slopes.

There is one climber[1] which bears growths that have the appearance of halberds. I never succeeded in finding out the function or
the purpose of these adornments. The plant is a liana of incredible
length, which climbs from tree to tree right to the top, often over
fifty metres up, to find the sun. Throughout its upward twists and
turns the diameter of the stem remains the same, not more than five
centimetres. From top to bottom it puts out shoots of varying
lengths which hang straight down and it is on these that the halberds appear. Green at first, the growths dry almost to black. They
are neither leaves nor spines and they have no apparent function
but to grace the shoots that carry them. I measured some of the
shoots which are very pliable; they taper a little, but are almost fili-
form, varying in size from half a metre to 1·2 metres long, with a
diameter of three centimetres at the base. Around each of these
shoots or spikes, the 'halberds' are arranged with absolute sym-
metry, in opposite pairs, each pair set at right angles to the previous
pair. The 'wings' of the halberds are not more than three centimetres wide, and the overall length of each pair is about six
centimetres.

Among the lianas are some valued by the islanders because they
provide a clear liquid which has a pleasant, rather bitter, vegetable

---

[1] The author gives no name for this climber, which has been tentatively identified
from the description as the rattan, or climbing palm.

taste. The liquid content of these stems is so great that it makes them extremely heavy to carry. These lianas are very common all over the islands and anyone who knows them need never die of thirst. To get at the liquid one only has to break the stem and put it to one's mouth; if one puts a receptacle under the break, a litre or so of liquid can be obtained in a matter of minutes. When the first strangers came to the archipelago, the Andamanese watched them tear down parts of the forest, including these lianas, and tried in vain to protest at the vandalism. No one understood their protests, but they were right.

The forest abounds in trees whose fruits in season form an important source of food for the islanders. One is the so-called jack-fruit, *Artocarpus communis*, which here grows wild, though various species are cultivated all over Asia. The fruits, which appear on the thickest branches as well as on the trunk, are smaller in the wild variety, rarely weighing more than thirty grams, but the yield is enormous and the islanders enjoy them for months, especially from March to May. The Onges call them *bulundanghe*, and roast them in hot ashes till the hard pulp and seeds are eatable; the latter, the size of a hazelnut but tougher, are the best part.

Another useful plant is the *Pandanus*, or screw-pine. On Little Andaman extensive areas are covered with nothing else, making progress very difficult owing to the twisting roots and the spines on the long, tough leaves. It seems to prefer the coastal areas, particularly the marshes, where it often grows into an impenetrable jungle. There are at least two species, one of which is gregarious. The other, which grows as isolated specimens, is longer leaved, with bigger fruits and stems like candelabra, standing up on an arch of roots, as though on stilts. With the leaves of this variety, fluted and easy to arrange like roof tiles, the Onges can quickly improvise a waterproof covering. The young leaves provide them with ornaments which they wear for their dances, while the pulp of the fruit, which looks rather like a pineapple, perfumed and delicately flavoured, is nutritious though somewhat stringy.

Along the coasts where there are no *Pandanus*, one very often sees something very different – mangroves. The islanders use the wood for their canoe floats, and for fixing pegs (see p. 122) and the supply is unlimited, as the growth and spread of the mangroves are assured by a number of factors which have made them one of the best adapted trees for the waterlogged areas in which they are exclusively found. The banks of all the river mouths and a considerable distance upstream are lined with the green of the mangroves, their trunks rising from the arched network of roots.

In the Andamans there are at least ten mangrove forests, all fighting for one thing: more and yet more vital space. This they win either directly, by sending roots out underground far ahead, or indirectly, by encouraging the building up of more land, which they then occupy. Great banks of mud are built up against the network of roots, sometimes miles into the sea, a necessary prelude to their irresistible spread. To help the formation of the dam mud some species send a mass of roots down from the trunk into the water, while others build dams of roots or send out horizontal shoots from which trunks sprout into the air and roots plunge down into the water.

One strange habit interested me very much. I saw roots thirty or more centimetres long growing not down but up, sticking into the air like a human hand with long fingers. These roots are known to botanists as 'pneumatophores', and the species which produce them act as the advance party for other species, building up a new plantation and snatching a few more miles from the sea. One might call it a fine example of solidarity among different species.

In these species tufts hang down from the leaves like green fingers about eighteen centimetres long. They are in fact great viviparous seeds, admirably adapted to progressive spread over marine areas, designed specifically for the purpose of sure and rapid growth wherever they alight, which may be anywhere. Floating upright in the sea, sticking half out of the water, their weight is so distributed that the growing tip is clear and the seeds take root the moment they arrive in shallow waters where there is mud below. The new plant grows rapidly, sending out miniature pneumatophores almost as soon as it has taken root.

In species like the well-known *Rhizophora conjugata* the seed germinates while still on the parent plant. If it does not become detached at once it sends out slender but strong roots a metre long. They too will float on the water until they can take root in the mud.

With all these means of propagation, even the fury of the sea is not enough to restrain the growth of the mangrove swamps. Slowly and unaided they are increasing the area of the islands with their arched vaults of roots, strong enough to bear a man's weight without bending. In some places I had to travel hundreds of metres across them, clambering from arch to arch, before I could reach dry land and sweeter air (the air in the swamps is foul with the stench of dead fish, crustacea and debris of all kinds from the sea, caught in the network of roots). Among the roots swarm crabs of all kinds, including the blue crabs, while kingfishers and other brilliantly coloured birds dart gaily in after the easy prey.

Near the mangrove swamps, in the mouths of the rivers, giant fronds of the Nipah palm stick up out of the water here and there. The feathery fronds, standing several metres high, are used by the crabs to climb out of the water and tiny toad fish, (see p. 133) equipped with both gills for life under water and lungs for air breathing, like to cling to them for an airing when there are no stones handy. Every day these fascinating little creatures stay in the sun for hours before dropping back into the waters of the swamps and in some places they are everywhere, always ready to jump out of the water on to a convenient projection to have a look at what is going on.

The Andamans, with their luxurious growth of vegetation of all kinds, are an ideal place to study plant dispersal. I have already mentioned the *Ficus* and the mangroves, but there are many other equally fascinating plants. Some used by the Onges for the production of fibres are widely distributed from India to Malaysia and the Pacific. Among these are *Gnetum gnemon* and *G. macrocarpum*, generally spread by the doves which flourish undisturbed on Little Andaman. In April, when the winds come, swarms of curious elongated parachutes equipped with an air trap which causes their spinning flight are blown from *Pterocarpus dalbergoides*, which provides the well-known *padàk* wood. The weight of the seeds (the size of a pea) at the base of the parachutes and the effects of the air trap give them a horizontal, screwing flight which carries them far from the parent tree. I have seen these parachutes in the sea, hundreds of kilometres from the nearest land. Mathematically designed by Nature to trap the right amount of air, the tiny parachutes are barely ten centimetres long. Their efficiency is self-evident – *padàk* is one of the most widely spread trees in the archipelago, in the Nicobars and far beyond.

In the stagnant pools on Little Andaman I found a species of explosive fungus which closely resembles, if it is not in fact identical with, its European counterpart. The spores, attached to a plume barely visible to the naked eye but wonderfully constructed, are carried into the sky by the air currents rising from the pools in the hottest part of the day and travel considerable distances.

One could fill whole books with the botany of the islands but here I can record only a few examples. One I cannot leave out is a species of *ipomea*, or Morning Glory, which flourishes on the sandy beaches in the lee of the coral reefs. The local varieties are not climbers, but spread over the ground in a compact lattice of stems, fairly well able to withstand the onslaught of wind and water. They prevent coastal erosion, both by the protection which their covering of strong stems and leathery leaves provides and by holding fast loose pieces of coral. These *ipomeas* are found only in the Andamans, some with purplish flowers and others white. They surround the communal huts along the coast, carpeting every free inch of ground cleared by the Onges of other and more destructive vegetation. They make no attempt to cut down the *ipomea*, as the compact growth helps their canoes to slide up and down the beach.

Along the coast of Little Andaman one sees rows of beautiful casuarinas (the Whistling Pine) especially a little to the north of Bugong Creek. From out at sea they stand against the skyline like rows of Italian cypress. They never reach the height of which they are capable, owing to the wind and the nature of the terrain; apart from a small stony, hilly area in the interior, of ancient continental origin, the island is really nothing more than a huge coral bank lying against these hills, which in the course of thousands of years has become covered with vegetal mould of no great depth. Trees are therefore forced to send their roots out horizontally, and the strong monsoon winds can easily uproot the tallest of them. After every storm one sees huge trunks lying on the ground, their wide net of roots sticking high into the air. Only a few of the giants in the interior manage to resist, protected by their neighbours. On Great Andaman, where there is more land of continental origin, deep rooting is possible and the forest presents a very different picture.

Much has already been written by others about the epiphytes, among them beautiful ferns and even more lovely orchids, which cling desperately to the trees in their struggle to reach the light. All are closely related to the flora of Burma, Malaysia, and Sumatra,

and particularly of Oceania, but not with that of the Indian peninsula – a fact which is highly significant in any reconstructive study
of the migration of flora and fauna to the archipelago.

The most recent phase in the spread of vegetation within the
Andamans is less than a hundred years old; it began on Great
Andaman, but none of the species has yet reached Little Andaman.
The coconut has reached it during the last few years, but when I
was there, there were not more than five wild palms in the whole
island. The original coconuts must have floated from Great Andaman, or even the Nicobars. The Onges at once realized that they
were edible, and called them *marele*. Now, however, there is a
plantation of over five hundred trees to the north of Labanar,
which I established by degrees on a number of occasions as a gift
to the Onges.

The absence of any cultivated plants on Little Andaman led me
to try pawpaws and bananas, as well as coconuts. In 1952 the
Governor himself suggested a plant whose leaves are said to cure
ringworm, so widespread among the Onges. The Onges, however,
were not remotely interested, nor were they any more interested
in the pawpaws and bananas. The pawpaws were left to lie on the
ground and groves of young plants sprang up, far too close together, crowding the original tree and not sturdy enough to fruit.
It was useless to show the Onges what to do. The bananas would
have grown well, but their leaves were ripped to pieces by the
storms. Possibly they would fare better in Great Andaman, where
the hills would afford some shelter from the wind.

A rather different result, but equally unfortunate, followed the
importation of grass seed into Great Andaman to improve grazing.
The seed, imported from Europe, must have been contaminated
with *Mimosa pudica*, which has spread widely, as it did in India and
the rest of southern Asia, and within a few years has destroyed the
grass so widely and become so much of a pest that in some areas
it is doubtful whether it can be eradicated. The area round Port
Blair is full of it, but for the moment Little Andaman remains free.

Culturally, the peoples of the Andamans remain today, unlike their
kin in Malaysia and the Philippines, at a level almost identical with
that of their ancestors thousands of years ago. They represented
then, and in great measure represent today, a pure hunting and

THE ANDAMAN ISLANDERS

gathering society; it is extremely probable that a study of their
daily life today is virtually equivalent to a study of their life as it
was in ancient times.

So near are the Andamanese to their original state that they show
no signs of ever having had any real agriculture. The Indian
Government has tried in vain to induce the surviving Arioto to
keep chickens by presenting them with birds and food for them;
the gifts were accepted out of politeness, but there the matter ended.
Among the remaining Negritos, however, particularly in the
Philippines, there are noticeable signs of the awakening of some
agricultural sense, even to the extent of some commerce, and
regular attendance at markets. But on Little Andaman, for example,
I saw in 1952 various ginger trees growing, brought there by some
unknown means and at Entigheh there was also a pumpkin. In
1953 and subsequent years there were no pumpkins at all on the
island, and although the gingers were still thriving they were
clearly doing so by chance, without any attention from the Onges,
who ate some of the small red fruit, and seemed to like the piquant
flavour, but still showed no signs of wanting to perpetuate it. In
several places both on the coast and inland I saw, too, clumps of
the slender native bamboo, hardly planted intentionally; the
ground sites of some huts now abandoned, like Bugheneh and
Odadda, were covered in them. The inhabitants had apparently
wanted to procure a supply of material for roofing mats, or the
drying platforms used by a few groups, and so the plantations were
completely stripped – and killed.

In order to plant coconut trees for the benefit of the islanders I
had even to do the planting myself, so utterly ignorant were they
of agricultural methods; we even had to do all the clearing of the
undergrowth in a patch of forest, and prepare the ground. The
Onges watched curiously but were quite uninterested. Why should
they care for a tree for ten years to get its nuts when the island and
seas around are teaming with food for the taking?

In their continual search for food the Onges have acquired
botanical and zoological knowledge which seems almost innate,
and they know of properties in plants and animals of which we are
quite unaware. Nearly every day on Little Andaman I came across
examples of this. I only had to draw a rough sketch of an animal
and they knew at once where it could be found; it was only thanks

to them that I was able to find the various amphibia which subsequently proved to be new species. They know poisonous and non-poisonous snakes by sight and how to avoid being bitten. They could tell me which trees flowered and when, because they knew this affected the whereabouts and the quality of the honey, and they knew which flowers and roots had medicinal properties. The necessity, in accordance with their superstitions, of keeping their prey alive as long as possible has also given them a somewhat gruesome knowledge of anatomy and physiology. The call of food has also made them weather experts; they know which air currents and winds bring what animals, or cause them to vanish, and what game is likely to haunt what terrain. They could tell me where to find certain fish, or crustacea, or where certain roots or fruit in season were to be found.

The striking feature of their knowledge was that it did not merely relate to what was edible or inedible. Amphibia, reptiles and birds for example, they never eat under any circumstances; but they knew where to find them all for me, and they knew the bird migrations and how these related to the movements of the marine fauna.

Providentially, the exactitude of the Onges' botanical and zoological knowledge is matched by the magnitude of their superstitious fears. Were it not for this all the edible vegetation on the islands would have disappeared long ago as a result of their incredibly thoughtless destruction. The effect, therefore, is almost that of a purely involuntary, embryonic form of 'agriculture', contrasting strangely with their persisting, persistent and complete lack of interest in any formal care, however primitive. The Onges believe that the plants which produce edible roots and tubers belong to a spirit related to Eiuga, whose anger is aroused if he sees his plants being taken; his vengeance is quick and terrible.

There are on Little Andaman a number of creepers with edible fleshy roots, sometimes as thick as a man's wrist, sticking out horizontally at least fifty to sixty centimetres from the main stem, only just below the surface. They invariably grow in light soil, where there are no rocks, and are very easy for the Onges to reach with their digging sticks. These and the yams, sometimes as big as a football, which are to be found everywhere, the Onges have to steal from the spirit who owns them. The creepers themselves, twining up into the trees, and the shorter-stemmed yams, are never disturbed. The Onges merely dig down, at a respectful distance from the plant, certain of finding what they want. On no account must there be any signs of the theft for the spirit to see, so they quietly take off roots or tubers some way from the main stem and leave the rest, patting the earth down afterwards and covering the place with leaves. The guardian spirit, not, apparently, all-seeing, notices nothing, as the plant continues to flourish, improved by the root pruning. Everyone, guardian spirit and Onges alike, is happy.

This unconscious preservation may well be the result of a decree, in some remote past, by an Onge seer who realized the danger of killing off the entire plants and invented the guardian spirits as a deterrent. The Negritos still make similar use of roots and tubers; Skeet and Blagden fifty years ago referred to the Semang eating poisonous wild yams, having removed the toxic substances.[1]

It is interesting that both in the past and even today a number of peoples at a very early stage of cultural development have progressed from the gathering of the wild yams of South-East Asia to the first signs of cultivation and agriculture. It is possible that they were the first plants ever to be cultivated by primitive Man, the Negritos with their digging sticks delving then as they do now; the genus is certainly a very ancient one, and some species, such as *Dioscorea alata*, may have spread from Asia to Africa and Oceania, and even to America, with the beginning of cultivation. But this is a stage of development which the peoples of the Andaman never reached.

The digging stick, the only implement the Onges have with which to get at the roots and tubers, has in recent times been affected, though to a very limited extent by the spread of iron. Only a few individuals possess a primitive iron tool, half a metre long, cylindrical in shape and usually not more than one and a half centimetres in diameter and flattened into a form of blade at one end. The vast majority still have only the age-old stick made of hard wood, hardly recognizable as a tool and crudely fashioned into a point at one end. This tool, so primitive that it can easily be mistaken for an odd

[1] It is interesting that the American Aborigines, especially in Brazil, do the same with manioc, but I saw nothing of this nature in the Andamans.

38

piece of wood, has definite uses, and none of the nomadic forest peoples anywhere in the world are without it. Everywhere it is found it is effective in filling huge baskets with food – baskets equally simply and equally quickly made. I have already described (see p. 93) the baskets made by the Onges for purely temporary use on their hunting expeditions. In the communal huts, however, the making of real baskets involves hours of careful plaiting, working the supple fibres from the strong bark of selected rushes, and expert finishing. These baskets are an invariable and prized part of every family's inheritance and are preserved for as long as possible. Nowhere in the collection of basketry from Great Andaman are there baskets with more craftsmanship than the permanent ones of the Onges.[1] All the baskets are the shape of half an egg. There is little variation in size, all being about forty centimetres in diameter at the top, and about forty-five centimetres deep, unlike the temporary carriers, which vary considerably in size, according to whether they are to be carried by men, women, or even children, and what is to be carried.

At the opposite extreme from the underground harvest of roots, men and women alike use long thin hooked poles to hook down fruit from the trees, climbing up into the trees when necessary to strip the highest branches and then hiding the poles in the forest until they are next required (no attempt is ever made to carry them about). When the tree is not too large, it is ruthlessly chopped down and stripped as it lies on the ground. I was horrified in the first fortnight of April to see this happen to trees which the Onges call *dangheccio*, which bear blackish-red fruit about the size of a pigeon's egg. The attraction is the flavour of the pulp, but there is little of it, surrounding a large nut. To get at the pulp a thick, hard case has to be cracked, but to the formidable Onge teeth this is no problem and the case cracks comparatively easily. The nut itself is not edible; the honey-coloured pulp is sweetish, but there is so little that it takes ten fruits to provide ten grams of it. The fruits hang in bunches at the end of branches covered with leaves rather like a chestnut. As the wood is very soft, the Onges usually hack the trees down; large ones may merely have their branches lopped

[1] Editor's note: The author indicated in manuscript at this point his intention of giving a full description of the way in which these are made, but unfortunately died before he was able to do so.

39

off, so that they may eventually recover, although they may take several years to do so.

The fruit they gather most, however, is the *bulundanghe*, a wild form of the so-called jack-fruit. This ripens a little later than the *dangheccìò* at the end of April, and is the occasion of intense activity. Men, women and children swarm to the harvest, returning to the camp loaded every night. When fully ripe the *bulundanghe* fall open if rubbed between the fingers. I found the pulp very pleasant, but the seeds need the Onge stomach to cope with them. They would in fact be suitable for storage over long periods as they do not seem to deteriorate, but the Onges would never think of this.

At no other time of year did I see so many baskets lying round the Onge camps, cast aside after use. As early as mid-March, impatient for the fruit, bitter but already fully grown to the size of a child's head, the Onges begin to strip the trees. When fully ripe the fruit are a yellowish-green, with a very wrinkled outer case, marked off as it were into tiny compartments, geometrical in shape, and mostly pentagonal. If one presses a finger on one of these it goes through into the fruit, which has the appearance of innumerable tiny cells, all separated by a membrane, each terminating in a seed at the central core of the fruit. The cells are an orange-yellow on the surface, becoming a very pale yellow inside when the pulp becomes softer. The seeds are covered by a sweetish orange skin, and are arranged regularly along the core, which is itself an extension of the stout, woody stalk.

The best parts to eat are the seeds and their sweetish skin. When the fruits are still unripe, sour, and hard, enormous quantities have to be gathered and carried to the camp where they are boiled until they are soft enough to open. The seeds are taken out and all the rest of the fruit is thrown away. When properly ripe, on the other hand, the seeds in their skins can be extracted on the spot, leaving the weight of the useless residue behind, lying in heaps under the tree. For eating, the skins are slit open with a *Cyrena* shell, the seeds extracted, and the skins and seeds piled up separately on huge leaves. The leaves are then tied up with the usual cords of vegetable fibres, and the bags laid on hot ashes. The skins turn into a sticky paste, not bad tasting, and the roasted seeds are greatly improved to our taste, though still very indigestible.

In April and May the Onges eat *bulundanghe* morning, noon and night. Everything else stops. *Bulundanghe* are food enough, and even honey is left for the future; there will be larvae, and bees, and nests to come. Life is good!

Later come the large, heavy *Pandanus* (*Mane* to the Onges) but they are far less important. The whole fruit has hardly any smell, but immediately it is open it smells rather like a pineapple. The separate segments, actually carpals, each in its own skin, pineapple-coloured on the outside shading to a pale yellow, can be picked off one by one. Each carpal is rather like a pyramid, with the top towards the centre of the fruit, the base towards the outside, wrinkled and divided into cellules each containing an ovule. The edible part of the fruit is very small. In the Nicobars, where the huge cultivated variety can weigh anything up to two kilos, the women spend hours passing a string through and through the heavy sphere of orange pulp to comb out the short bristly fibres which damage the stomach. The Onges are not interested in such niceties! The smaller wild fruit is merely broken into pieces, ready for chewing. The result of all the chewing is hardly worth the effort; there is taste, and there is smell, but the food value is very small indeed, and even the Onges seem to realize it.

Much better are the *gioghene*, which ripen in February, and the *ghine* in mid-March. The *gioghene* are soft, red fruit, the size of a cherry but rather less rounded, hanging in bunches from the trunk and the larger branches of the tree. The green seed sprouts out of the end of the fruit, like a large bean, but is not eaten; the Onges cut it off, and eat only the pulpy fruit, raw. They love to make necklaces, twining the fruits with slender fibres into long garlands, even making some for me when I was with them, and return to the camp every night with long ropes hanging round their necks and from their arms.

Ghine are very different. From the outside they look like small medlars, covered with a leathery skin which is easy to crack off with one's teeth. The fruit itself has three segments, and is rather gelatinous, a little sour, but quite edible. The Indians with me liked them very much and ate so many that they developed severe indigestion – unlike the Onges, who ate far more with no ill effects.

CHAPTER THREE

The Spirits of the Forest

It is only too easy to get lost in the forests, but this never happens with the Onges. They do not rely upon the 'mysterious sense of direction' which is often attributed (without adequate evidence) to primitive peoples; they have other simpler but equally effective ways of finding their way. Everywhere the Onges go they leave behind some mark. When they come to a halt in the depths of the forest, they cast around them, and soon find signs leading to some temporary shelter or communal hut.

As the Onges are out in the forest every day, there are traces of their passage everywhere. Inconspicuously broken plants, or scratches on the branches of trees are precious marks, one leading to the next and so on to the camp. Everyone takes care not to get lost, and moves carefully through the sea of vegetation, without appearing to mark their way. I have often been surprised to find myself back at the camp after innumerable twists and turns, but the Onges' exceptional eyesight saved us when the situation seemed to me quite hopeless.

They were always able, too, to calculate exactly how far to go in one stage, and could invariably tell me precisely when we should arrive at a given point. They have no form of clock and work solely by the sun's position. But whatever their method, every time I asked when we should reach a certain camp, they always replied at great length: they would point with one outstretched arm to *Tenculu* the Sun and then with the other to where it would be when we arrived. The passing of days was indicated by moving an arm from east to west, saying *Tenculu – Tenculu,* to show sunrise and sunset. It was a simple matter to work out what they meant, and their answer was invariably right.

Owing to the difficulty of pushing through the undergrowth the Onges always travel in single file, following closely behind one another, the men first, then the women and children, with the dogs following all round. They never travel alone; I hardly ever met any by themselves, but always in groups of families or groups of hunters. The man who happens to be at the front of the file is the guide and when they come to an awkward part of the journey – perhaps across a deep river – everybody helps. Trees are felled to fall across between the banks and a rope of lianas is run across to make the crossing easier for the aged, the women and the children, though their sense of balance is so good that most of them manage without it, even when carrying heavy loads across a single trunk.

The Onges are now nearly all related to each other in some way. They all know each other, and the contacts are usually friendly. The few squabbles which I saw, always over game, or food that had been gathered, all blew over very quickly; normally, especially in the dry season when every group becomes nomadic in search of food, everyone went freely all over the island. On the occasions of the great hunts, or the honey feasts, a number of groups would band together for the occasion and even then they tried to divide the spoils equally and peaceably. If a dispute does arise the camp will break up into factions, but these will still keep close to each other and after a short while their differences will be made up with the usual long and tearful embraces. These scenes of reconciliation may go on for days, all starting from nothing more serious than a difference of opinion over the division of game captured by communal effort!

Much more important than the danger of offending other human beings is that of causing offence to the spirits of the dead or the guardian spirits who provide food. There is, as I have said, not over-much rigidity in their observations – no propitiatory offerings of any kind are made to the spirits. The supreme being, Eiuga, who takes the shape of a lizard bigger than a crocodile, they know well. On Great Andaman he becomes Puluga, equally powerful, lord of men and things but rather more anthropomorphic than his counterpart in Little Andaman. As Eiuga lives in the sky, the thunder is his voice, and the wind his breath; if he is angry he breathes out storms and throws burning tree-trunks down to the earth, setting light to the forest. Behind Eiuga are a series of minor spirits who rule the multiplication and growth of the various animals and plants useful to Man.

The Onges do not love Eiuga, or any of the other spirits. They merely fear them, and seek to evade their anger by various expedients. It is curious that they never hesitate to try and deceive the spirits and think themselves very clever when they manage to steal roots or tubers from the ground. Nor do they revere the spirits of their ancestors; these are to be feared and propitiated by preservation of their bones. By definition none of the spirits, since they can be deceived by simple tricks, can be all-powerful, but this conclusion, simple though it is, is still beyond the Onges' powers of reasoning.

The Onges' fear of the dead is instanced by their carrying round their necks the *ibidanghe*, or necklet of human jaws, as a propitiation. The wearing of the bones prevents the spirit from going away (by analogy the bones of dead enemies are burned to force the spirit, clearly a hostile one, to leave the place). The custom of burial within the communal hut follows the same logic – the spirits of the dead are kept near their bones and hence near their relatives, to help them in the daily round of hunting, fishing and gathering food.[1]

Unlike most of the other peoples whose burial customs are even today based on their underlying principles, the Onges have not progressed beyond the stage of relating the dead directly to the demands of daily life; they have no 'practices' of any kind, no concept at all of holy places, prayers or images. Even the very names of the dead are soon forgotten. Their fears, however, are none the less very real. They do not like to speak of Eiuga or even of the lesser spirits, for fear of attracting their attention.

The Onges have no stories or explanatory legends, like those reported by Brown for Great Andaman. They have only short epics, if such they may be called, recalling extraordinary events in

---

[1] This belief is of very remote origin, and can be traced back at least to the megaliths of southern Asia, like the splendid ones which I was able to photograph, among others, in the mountains of Travancore. Here again the object was to prevent the dead from leaving their relatives. Similar ideas are found today in India among several tribes, notably the Munda, or Nias, and among various peoples of Indonesia, and even Oceania. The rituals are probably followed today without any understanding of their meaning or symbolism; the details vary from place to place, but the underlying principle, the original fear, remains the same everywhere.

their hunting and fishing, or contacts with strangers, which are loudly chanted, accompanied by miming and dancing, during their nocturnal celebrations. One was sung and danced in my honour; Cendubai,[1] head of the Lulera hut, much struck by the sight of me in my hammock slung between two trees on nylon cords, delivered himself of a warning over the danger I was running using such thin cords. At the end of each 'verse' the refrain '*cué-cian-ghéghechée-chéle*' (he will hurt himself) repeated his fear of the cords breaking.

Hunting and fishing episodes are to the Onges less interesting than themes like my safety, because to them they lack the repetitive refrain. In their dances, on the other hand, they prefer something else, to us monotonous, but for them always new, and even exciting; more than anything they love to dance the stages of courtship to its culmination, with the help of words and extraordinarily (to Western eyes regrettably) vivid gestures.

Birds, to the Onges, harbour the spirits of the dead, and it is for this reason that they are never eaten, contrary to the assertions of Brown.[2] Similar fears extend to lizards, the jungle cats, bats, rats and snakes. I have confirmed this among both the Onges and the Arioto. The latter even refused to eat some fat pigeons which I offered them not knowing of the taboo; they accepted the gifts, but the pigeons were eventually eaten by my own men. And the Onges whom I took with me to Port Blair for a few days refused point blank to eat pigeon or chicken.

The spirits select the Onges' food for them, in the sense that they regard everything as edible or poisonous, according to whether the guardian spirit is benign or malevolent. Given the curious adaptability of the spirits and the intensely practical way in which they operate it is hardly surprising that their benevolence or malignity coincides remarkably well with those foods which tend to promote normal health!

[1] I was sorry to learn that Cendubai died suddenly in 1955 aged barely forty.

[2] Curiously enough, while the Onges' fears lead them to reject out of hand any food of animal origin which is unknown to them, the same does not apply to vegetable foods. They ate half-rotten fruit, which I offered them, even though they had never seen it before, and they clamoured for rice and tea, so much so that in order to prevent them becoming addicted to the rice, as so often happens when primitive peoples meet a new food, I insisted on receiving equal quantities of yams in exchange for the rice and very sweet tea, to slow down their demands.

To truly primitive peoples like the Onges, European medical practices are fascinating. Men and women will refuse literally nothing once they are convinced of our intention to do them good and cure their ills. Although they have a rudimentary form of medicine, they recognize the superiority of European methods, and medical aid has therefore become our most powerful means of making contact with uncivilized peoples.

While I was busy trying to alleviate their ailments I became aware of the power which 'medicine' has over them, and I was also able to observe their own methods of dealing with their ills. Understandably, disease, death and birth are all attributed to particular supernatural beings, or to the spirits of the dead. They try not to offend these beings, but strive nevertheless, in their own way, at least to cure disease. Once primitive peoples see our methods they respect them, and are eager to be treated; strange though it all seems, they develop a blind faith in the omnipotence of the new ways.

There is little actual disease among the Onges and they have equally few vices. They are still unaware of the existence of alcohol, and have not learned how to ferment sugar substances, such as the honey in which the Little Andaman abounds. Tobacco is a recent introduction, and the Onges at once became wildly addicted to it; the tobacco leaves I had taken with me were in fact my best means of making my way peacefully into the island. A few Onges have acquired a supply of opium from Burmese and Chinese smugglers along the north coast, but instead of smoking it they seem to limit themselves to chewing it mixed with tobacco, and have fortunately no means of replenishing their stock.

Polio, tuberculosis, smallpox and cancer seem unknown, but for some unknown reason the islands have on a number of occasions been struck by disastrous epidemics of measles. These epidemics struck nearly every member of some of the communal huts, judging from survivors' reports, and the sites were afterwards abandoned, leaving the huts to be destroyed by termites.

The census of 1931 includes a personal observation by Portman of congenital syphilis in several Onges. This has since been proved wrong and in 1952 I found only one young man with nasal malformation possibly attributable to the disease, half-moon incisors, and abnormality of the skull and palate. I was not able to find him on later visits. Dr H. Lehmann found no evidence of syphilis in the fifty-two individuals of both sexes from whom he took blood samples in my presence.

Although the Onges are normally healthy and look outwardly robust, they have very little actual resistance to disease and succumb very quickly. Twenty-eight of them, whole families, young and old, whom I took with me to Port Blair in 1954 to present them to the President of the Republic of India, all developed a high fever owing to the change in their way of life during the few days it took from Little Andaman to Great Andaman, and we had to take them back hastily to their own island immediately after the official visit. Even minor feverish complaints of no importance seem to depress and terrify them so that they die very quickly, and I sometimes heard that young Onge friends whom I had left in excellent health had died suddenly from, so I was told, some febrile complaint. The Onge women have better resistance than their menfolk to disease as a whole, which may also help to explain their greater longevity.

On the other hand wounds heal surprisingly quickly in both sexes, although in some of the old men I saw purulent leg sores, slow to heal even when treated with antiseptics which I applied myself. I saw none of these in women, but they seem to be more severely attacked by ringworm, especially on the abdomen and round the umbilicus. Few of the Onges were free from ringworm but none of them bothered to treat it, and it did not seem to cause them any noticeable disturbance. In one woman I noticed whitish patches on the fingers and lips, due to leucoderma.

Diseases of the nervous system and mental illnesses seem very rare, although a few individuals are subject to attacks of epilepsy, watched reverently by all present! The Onges regard epileptics as possessed by a spirit capable of giving important information and question them like the oracle. A number of the Onge leaders, among them Giota of Tambe-e-buiè, go from time to time into a state of trance, which has every appearance of an epileptic attack. I saw one case of dementia in a middle-aged woman, but it was mild enough to allow her to go about her work reasonably well, and at regular intervals she produced normal children.

Sight and hearing in the Onges are particularly acute, as has often been reported in primitive peoples and attributed to the regular exercise of the two faculties required by their existence in direct contact with the natural world; anyone, it is said, who lived such a life would preserve the same keenness of eye and ear. Certainly I saw no myopia among the Onges, nor any of the eye infections common among other inhabitants of the tropics. With the naked eye they can pick out tiny craft far out to sea, or the small, narrow Onge canoes which I could hardly see with field-glasses, which makes me doubt whether constant exercise of the eyes can really be the full explanation of their power of vision. They can pick out quickly and accurately birds immobile among the dense leaves in the darkest part of the forest, invisible to me, even though I was used to looking for them and could see them when they moved. And from the ground they saw high in the trees tiny amphibia which I wanted to catch, after I had caught one by chance which had proved to be a new species. These amphibia, perfect mimics, become almost invisible when they attach them-selves to the bark of the trees, but the Onges pointed them out to me from a distance with absolute accuracy, and I was in fact able in 1954 to catch over two hundred in a week.[1]

The Onges can also pick out reptiles on the ground, or among the foliage, distinguishing with long practice the poisonous varieties which abound in the islands, and I found it very useful to send Onges ahead of me in the forest to look out for these snakes. When any of my Indians were bitten it was always because they thought they could do as well as the local scouts! The Onges them-selves are, however, occasionally bitten, with serious consequences. One of them, aged twenty-five, climbed into a very high tree after honey, and unwittingly put his left hand on a snake hidden in the leaves, where it had climbed to search for birds' eggs. It bit just above the elbow, causing an alarming swelling of the arm with severe pain and fever. He was brought to me semi-conscious, with the whole limb swollen to the size of a rugby ball. The unfortunate man's neck had been bound with the usual strands of *Ficus* bark, and not surprisingly he was groaning desperately, and clearly on the point of death.

The Onges have no specific remedies for snake bites, and their

[1] These amphibia were examined in 1954 at the Institute of Zoology of the University of Genoa and given the name of *Kalcula baleata ghoshi*, in honour of Mr A. K. Ghosh, then Governor of the Andamans.

attempts to help, after binding his throat, had consisted in smearing the man's entire body with a mixture of ochre, turtle fat and honey with an extra layer on the bitten limb. Although it was very late to start treatment I injected antiserum, and the next day the man seemed a little better. I next saw him eleven days after the injection, when the arm appeared much less swollen, and the pain had almost disappeared, although clear traces of the accident remained; the skin was cracked and peeling, and the two puncture marks at the site of the bite were still gaping open, each revealing red, purulent flesh over a circular area more than two centimetres in diameter. The arm looked almost gangrenous, but its owner did not seem worried, and joined in cheerfully with the others round me. Just over a month after the accident the wound was completely healed, leaving one very grateful patient.

The incident shows the complete solidarity of this simple and reputedly so warlike community; by tacit agreement the patient was relieved of all work, and provided with food by the other families in the communal hut. While he was seriously ill his wife went hunting and fished, normally the man's work. Similar help is given in the case of the aged, or if a wife and mother falls ill; food is provided for them, and for the children, and certain 'soothsayers' appear to be at least partially provided with food by the rest of the community on a permanent basis.

For any kind of fever the Onges turn immediately to their stock remedy, smearing the entire body with the usual mixture of ochre, turtle fat and honey. The legs, arms, chest and abdomen are then tightly bound with strips of *Ficus* bark, which are removed and renewed from time to time. Whether the patient has pains in the abdomen or in the chest, or elsewhere, or has a cough, he is invariably stretched out on the ground, and the appropriate part is given a form of vigorous massage by the feet of one of the bystanders. Usually the entire body is pummelled for quite a time, the patient being turned over and over. The patient ends up looking rather like a mummy plastered in ochre and the whole process is to us somewhat amusing, but the Onges all practise it, and submit to it, very seriously, believing implicitly in its efficiency. The mechanism by which the treatment works has yet to be determined!

Balls of ochre the size of a hazelnut and varying in colour from bright red to whitish-yellow are given by mouth, particularly to children. I have seen anything up to half a dozen given, one after another. Their laxative effect is sometimes violent, as the ochre is mixed with the usual turtle fat, plus lumps of pure wax from the hives of the black bees.

Another 'cure' is the smoking of the affected part. One young woman well known to me, Nabinibbi (wife of Maritòi, leader of the Cemalè group), plump and in her own way graceful, had burnt two toes of her right foot, and was unable to sleep with the pain. She smeared the foot well beyond the burn with the usual mixture and held it out to the smoke of great fresh liana seeds laid among embers. The seeds, the size of a large chestnut, but lenticular and covered with a dark brown, leathery skin, burnt with a dense smoke.

Another treatment, rather different, was applied to one of my Onge guides, Toncutèi, who developed a high fever on the night of 28 March 1954, while he was in the communal hut known as Entiguèh, in the north-central area of the island. In fact, it was merely violent indigestion caused by too much pork – Toncutèi, like his father Enagaghe, an indefatigable trencherman, had availed himself too freely of the boars shot that day by my men. His friends laid him on his side on the ground on a rectangular mat barely large enough to take his body, with his legs bent up to his chest. They then lit low fires along two adjoining sides of the mat, turning him from time to time so that he 'cooked' evenly. One Onge began spitting on the patient's hair, and rubbing the spittle into the skin, stopping every now and again to press the victim's head between his hands. Another dissolved ochre in water, and after heating it, rubbed it well into the patient's chest, throat and neck. Meanwhile, a third beat his hands vigorously on Toncutèi's. This went on for just over a quarter of an hour, after which the patient was stretched out on his stomach with his feet sticking out over the end of the mat, ready for the foot massage. As the masseur's foot reached the chest he stopped, pressing hard to enforce complete emptying of the lungs. Half an hour of this led to further rubbing with hands and feet for another fifteen minutes, particularly over the sacrum. Finally Toncutèi was left in peace beside the fire. By dawn the fever was gone (aided possibly by the strong purgative I had administered), although it was a couple of days before he had fully recovered.

Near my camp at Labanar, in March 1952, I witnessed a distressing and fatal case. A young woman, with a baby a month old, had suckled another child, as the Onge women do. The older infant, which had cut its teeth, caused damage to the nipples and the ensuing infection spread throughout the body. The wretched woman was writhing with fever and the pain from her infected breasts and suppressed lactation. Her body had been smeared with a vermilion ochre, held to be the most powerful balm, and tightly bound, as usual. Her condition was so poor that I suggested sending her at once to Port Blair for treatment. Unfortunately, however, at that time I was only just beginning to establish contact with the Onges, and the woman's husband, after all the arrangements had been made, refused to let her go. I had not yet gained the Onges' confidence enough to be allowed near the woman, and although I was able to photograph her I could do nothing to prevent her death.

The decision to administer 'medicine' and subject patients to various treatments is not the province of any specialists, but is taken by anyone in the group; all, including the patient, accept the decision, since all are utterly convinced that it will benefit them. Medicine men and sorcerers, so numerous in Africa and elsewhere, do not exist among the Andamanese.

The Onges have not the slightest idea of any standards of hygiene. They never wash intentionally; the forest, dripping from every leaf, and frequent immersion in water while out hunting, take care of the problem. One must admit that in the circumstances their nakedness is hygienic. A small fire is kept burning beside each bed at night for warmth, a useful precaution which I found very welcome on the many cold nights which followed a very hot day. Deprived of these fires the Onges fall ill at once, a fact of which I had ample proof on several occasions when I took Onges with me out of Little Andaman; they were provided with beds and coverings in well-constructed wooden houses, but although none of them complained about the absence of the fires by their beds they all developed feverish chills.

And yet in their own territory I have seen them lie soaking wet all night in one of their temporary forest camps or a communal hut with a leaking roof without any ill effects, simply because they had their fires beside them. On the night of 4–5 April 1953, while I was sleeping with them in the communal hut at Berié-Abdalù a sudden storm drenched us all, forcing us to huddle together round fires under the more waterproof parts of the roof. Numb with cold, but cheerful, they began joking, singing[1] and dancing, men and women separately; this went on all night, and no one suffered any ill effects from the soaking.

The Onge lack of hygiene extends also to their cooking utensils, which are never washed. In recent years the ocean has provided the Onges with a generous and unexpected gift; currents running from the south of Asia have thrown up on to the shores of Little Andaman a shoal of empty petrol drums, stout metal cylinders 1·3 metres high and eighty centimetres in diameter. The astute Onges have patiently divided each one in two, each section big enough to take a large pig. Set on big fires these serve as wonderful cooking pots, and the Onges are delighted with them. Unfortunately, however, although they were thrown up all round the island, the supply is beginning to dry up, and they are rapidly being eaten away by rust.

To boil food, the Onges set the drums on two large logs, laid parallel, with a fire between them. Stones are rarely used to support the drums, although there are plenty about in the interior of the island. On the coast, and for a fair way inland, there is nothing but coral, hard but liable when it gets hot to disintegrate under the heavy weight of the cylinders filled to the brim.

In these gifts from the sea the Onges could prepare tasty broths, but they invariably allow nearly all the water to boil away, and the cooking process is not considered complete until all the liquid has gone. While it is boiling, however, they take care not to lose the fat floating on the top, which they adore. They have even invented a curious sort of dipping-stick for the purpose of skimming the fat off. They take a shoot about twenty centimetres long from a plant which disintegrates into fibre when chewed. One end is chewed into a loose 'brush' and no one present misses his turn to dip it into the pot again and again to skim off a mouthful of fat, even getting up in the night in their eagerness for it. One stick naturally does for everyone, men, women and children, the

[1] The Onge voice is not markedly different from the European. It has a musical quality, fairly high-pitched but never shrill; the Onges never raise their voices, even in anger – disagreements invariably end in a dignified silence.

mothers offering it to the waiting children one after another in strict order. This alone would be enough to explain the spread of the devastating measles epidemics which can attack every member of a hut.

While they love the liquid fat, they despise the broth left behind, and once the meat has been eaten, a thick yellowish soup, not unpleasant, is left in the drum. The dogs love this, and rush for it, putting their paws right into the drum, fighting and snarling in their eagerness to get at it. When they have finished licking, the drum is shining clean and ready for use, with no washing up to do! Clouds of flies descend on the drums, packing into a black swarm all over the bottom and sides, eager to finish off the dogs' work. Sea or river water is often only a yard or two from camp, but no one would dream of washing anything.

Once the meat or fish is cooked, it is often hung in the roof of the hut, out of reach of the dogs. The fact that the roof is dusty and covered in spiders to foul the meat, does not matter; earth and sand get in the way of the teeth, dust and spiders do not. The Onges happily eat contaminated flesh and drink water from pools in which animal carcasses are rotting or dogs are bathing and drinking; the dogs share literally everything with their masters.

On my visits to the island I always had to fence off the wells I had dug out, to avoid a constant battle with the dogs. I always found water only a few metres down, and the dogs revelled in it. In the east, near Nachuge, I saw Onges and dogs together avidly drinking in brackish pools which stank of sulphur, although I must confess that after repeated filtration and boiling the water lost its smell and I was myself able to use it without any ill effects. My men thought it was good for the health to drink it as it was.

During all Onge orgies, and particularly the honey feasts, there is, if possible, even less regard for hygiene. Although the honey is full of wax, larvae, and a few odd bees, their brush-stick only picks up the honey itself. They have another even better way of getting out the honey. A strip of bark about one metre long and as wide as the palm of the hand is taken from a *Ficus*. This is well chewed to make it pliable, and when this is dipped into the honey mixture it emerges dripping with pure honey. Everyone bites at it avidly, young and old, men, women and children, one after another, to the last drop.

Cleaning themselves, to the Onges, means painting themselves to ward off evil and to remove, so they said, the smell of pig fat after the colossal orgies which follow a particularly good hunt, when even they find the stench too much. These orgies, which give them appalling indigestion for days, are followed by an apparently instinctive variation of their diet to raw or cooked vegetable foods. On three occasions from 1952–54 I was present at one of these solemn pork and honey orgies. The Onges ate almost till they burst, and then, hardly able to move, cleaned up by a grand painting session. The women do the painting, families vying with each other to produce weird new designs, which are then copied until the next feast.[1]

Fed and painted, the Onges sit down to smoke, using pipes made from crabs' claws. Still regardless of hygiene the pipes go from one mouth to another, the women smoking just as heavily as the men.

One curious anomaly is that the Onges do sometimes sweep the earth floor of the communal hut. The floor is not deliberately beaten down, but becomes hardened by continuous walking on it; in dry weather it turns to dust, which rises and settles everywhere, especially under the roof, where the lumps of cooked meat, fish and so on are hung. For the cleaning a broom or besom is prepared, well made with very hard, supple, palm fibres, bound tightly and carefully with cords made from reeds. The whole thing is about eighty centimetres long and as thick as a man's wrist.

The dirt is simply swept out all round from under the roof of the hut through the gap between the roof and the ground. In the course of time a ring of refuse builds up round the hut, forming a glorious breeding ground for insects of all kinds. When the hut has to be rebuilt, owing to the ravages of wood-worm and termites, the ring is levelled off to form the new floor. Since the same small, well-chosen site may be used for thousands of years, the hut ends up perching on top of a small mound of refuse dating back to very

[1] From one year to the next I saw no real evolution of art forms but cyclic changes of designs, with a preference for certain geometric patterns, at certain times of the year. Having watched various individuals of both sexes closely over a period of some years I can say that in the Onges at least, contrary to what is generally understood, the use of given patterns, and given kinds of ochre, does not correspond with given types of food. Any feast is always followed by painting, always with the weirdest designs possible, but always geometrical, never far from the current 'fashion', and never even remotely inspired by the basis of the feast.

ancient times. Great Andaman abounds in these man-made humps, to which the name 'kitchen-middens' has been given, but none are in use today. In Little Andaman, on the other hand, many are still being built up.

The sweeping operations disturb clouds of flies and tiny beetles, light brown in colour, shot with metallic blue, with a highly domed back, and about five millimetres long, which always collect under bones and other human food refuse. Hordes of fleas, invisible in the dirt on the floor but multiplying busily, are also stirred up. Fortunately there are no lice on Little Andaman, owing to the absence of clothing and bed-linen, and the Onges carry no lice in their hair.

In fact the dogs' coats carry the fleas from place to place more than do their naked, smooth-skinned owners. Every time I went into a hut which had been empty for a time, as happens in the dry season when the occupants are away on a hunting trip, I was assailed by swarms of fleas such as I had never imagined! They rushed up one's body from feet to neck in absolute serried ranks, platoons of them, solid masses of tiny black moving objects. The only thing to do was to go out into the open and douse oneself in Flit, which caused them to retreat hastily. My camp-bed was always given a precautionary dose. Unfortunately Flit was not enough to disperse the clouds of ticks, tiny but dangerous, and a scourge in the forests of the Andamans. The Onges call them *anaghe* and thoroughly enjoyed helping to catch them on me in hundreds after every expedition into the forest.

None of these pests worry the Onges, who make no attempt to get rid of them. They leave mounds of filth round their huts or in their forest camps for them to breed in, and the light covering of earth or leaves which at best cover the Onges' faeces, deposited near the camp, was never any deterrent to breeding. The Onges never dig sanitary trenches or prepare any other form of latrines, even for their permanent sites; the forest is all concealing. However, they will never defaecate near, or in, a water course, even when the bed is dry, and when my men used the bed of a dried-up stream for the purpose the Onges protested to me, because the water would be contaminated. I was not disposed to contradict them.

In the forest, meeting a swarm of flies was a sure sign that we were approaching an Onge camp. Everywhere they go they are accompanied by flies of all sizes, and in Little Andaman the swarms are so bad that the first stranger to land called a river after them, Bumila Creek, or fly river. Their flies betray the Onges long before the barking of their dogs – no human voice ever betrays their silent presence.

On Little Andaman today the Onges' tacit divisions of territory are of little importance, so heavy has been the fall in population, but they still keep out of areas belonging to other 'huts', even if the huts themselves have been abandoned. I never saw any disputes over territory, or the ownership of the area in which a pig was caught (and hence ownership of the pig). The Onges who accompanied me, possibly encouraged by the prestige value of a European with them, hunted wherever we went without anyone raising any protests. Nevertheless, I always took the precaution of giving anything I or my Indians took to the Onges of the nearest hut, invariably much to their delight.

Contrary to established opinion, communal huts on Little Andaman are not found only along the coasts; the majority, and certainly the best constructed, are in the interior. Togalanghe is one, and there are a number of permanently abandoned temporary camps near it.

Both the permanent and temporary huts or shelters of the Andamans resemble those of the Semang. The latter are extremely simple, especially in the dry season; there are no walls and only a very sloping roof of leaves, high at the front and very low at the back, the beds being put so that the feet face the low part of the roof. With the Semang and Aeta the beds may be made of bamboo; this is never the case in the Andamans, as there are no large bamboos in the archipelago (Brown was wrong in this respect. The few slender bamboos on Little Andaman are only usable for making drying racks, which are found only round the hut at Beniaboi in the south. As the people were away when I went there, and the site was consequently completely deserted, I was unable to establish visually what they dried, but traces of fish, particularly pilchards, were indication enough.)

These temporary shelters are put up extremely quickly. Two poles less than two metres long for the front, and two more, thirty to forty centimetres long, for the back, are fixed firmly into the ground. Two parallel transverse poles of equal length, one front and one back, complete the frame, which is lashed together with the usual rush fibres. The roof consists of fresh *Pandanus* leaves, palms, or grass. It never actually touches the ground, and food refuse is thrown out from underneath it in the usual way, covering the ground round the shelter.

The bed takes a little longer than the roof to put up, as a number of sticks have to be gathered to make the compact platform, raised about half a metre from the ground on four stout props driven into the ground, one at each corner, and a suitable trunk has to be found for the head-rest. Normally one bed takes an entire family – mother, father, children and dogs, all well packed on the platform with the inevitable fire beside. On rare occasions, when the shelter is intended purely for the menfolk on a hunting expedition, only one bed is prepared, but generally every hunter has his family with him. I have myself slept like this with the Onges on trips where the forest was too dense for any baggage to be carried.

As the kitchen-middens show (see p. 68), their permanent huts are, with very few exceptions, circular and are still extremely simple. The essential feature is the waterproof roof-mats, well overlapped, which form the enormous umbrella roof. From the outside the whole thing looks in danger of collapsing, but from the interior it is obviously safely held by a frame of poles, lashed with innumerable ties to stout uprights fixed firmly into the ground. No central pillar is needed, and when there is one it is only by chance; I saw very few on Little Andaman. There are no divisions into rooms or compartments – everything is open to the eyes of all the occupants of the beds. Most of these are arranged as the radii of a circle, fairly near the outer edge of the hut, the roof coming down so close to the ground that everyone sleeps with their heads towards the centre, but there may be some beds across the centre space.

At the circumference the roof is only thirty to forty centimetres from the ground, the roofing mats being well lashed on to uprights in case of high winds, and one can wriggle in and out of the hut on one's stomach, crawling over the refuse thrown out through the convenient gap. There is always, however, a 'proper' entrance, where one edge of the roof-wall can be lifted up. At the top of the roof, on the lee side, one section can be propped open on poles, allowing the smoke to escape and letting more air in – a very welcome relief at times, even for the Onges!

I made sketch plans of all the huts I visited, with positions of the supporting poles, beds, etc. Two typical ones were those at Toqué-è-bùie and Tambe-e-buiè. In March 1952 the former had some parts of the roof missing, as the inhabitants had taken the mats off to make temporary shelters in the forest; when the rains came they brought them back and replaced them. This custom explained why, on Great Andaman, some obviously temporary shelters had roofs far too well made to be intended for purely temporary use.

Entering the hut at Toqué-è-bùie, by the entrance proper, one finds oneself facing an area with no beds in it. In the centre of this area, under the apex of the roof, is a fire, a little larger than those kept burning beside each bed. This is used for communal cooking during the rainy season; at other times all cooking is done in the open. The ground area covered by the roof was 9·12 square metres, its height at the centre 3·3 metres, and the external circumference 30·65 metres. Beyond this stretched the ring of refuse built up by each short period of occupation.

Unlike many of the huts of Little Andaman, Toqué-è-bùie has a central pole, not thick, but of a very hard wood. In a circle round this are ten upright poles, each about two metres from the central pole. Starting on the left of the entrance and moving clockwise their heights vary slightly.[1] Outside this inner circle of supporting poles are two more concentric rings of uprights, the first, with a radius of 3·65 metres from the central pole, consists of twenty uprights with an average height of 1·35 metres, and the second, with a radius of 4·53 metres from the centre pole, has an average height of 0·38 metres. In nearly every hut each circle of uprights is attached to the roof by a ring formed by a bundle of long canes, to which each upright is lashed. Another bunch of long canes runs transversely from the entrance to the opposite side of the hut, almost touching the ground at the two ends, touching the roof in the middle, and fixed to the rings of canes to which the uprights are attached.

The bundle of canes forming this arch support is clearly set in place after the erection of the first (innermost) ring of uprights, and actually lies on top of the ring of canes to which they are

[1] 2·45, 2·35, 2·32, 2·3, 2·45, 2·55, 2·3, 2·35, 2·32, 2·35 metres.

attached. From it to the ring run a series of long batons, the 'ribs' of the umbrella. All along the length of the transverse bundle of canes are attached the ends of similar 'ribs', with supplementary canes at weak points. In this hut and in a number of others, extra rings of canes not supported by uprights are put in afterwards for extra strength, all securely lashed at every point.

At this stage of construction the hut would thus have consisted of a centre pole, first circle of uprights supporting the first ring of canes, second (unsupported) ring of canes fixed to the 'ribs' running over it, second concentric circle of uprights supporting the third ring of canes, the fourth (unsupported) ring of canes, and the third circle of uprights supporting the fifth and last ring of canes. Right across from the entrance to the opposite side of the hut ran the elliptical transverse bundle of canes. Tight rush fibre lashings at every crossing and meeting point held the whole frame solidly together.

The roof itself was then put on. This consists of palm leaves like huge fans. The Onges split these in halves down the centre vein and then lay one half on top of the other, head to tail, main ribs together. Four, six or possibly more reeds, three metres long and two to three centimetres in diameter, are then split in half lengthwise and laid out parallel on the ground. The pairs of palm leaves are then laid across the parallels and lashed securely with rush fibres, working from the bottom up, so that the edges of each pair cover the ribs of the pair below, making a water-shed. Seen from the inside of the finished hut the ribs, blackened by smoke, look almost like parallel vaulting.

In this particular hut there are beds for seven families (and their dogs) set as radii, and four transversely. Round the centre pole, on three sides only (leaving the fourth open for access to the central fire) are three fairly high platforms, rather smaller than the beds. Occasionally I saw young people sleeping on two of these, very cramped, climbing up a fixed ladder to reach them. The third platform was always used to keep meat out of the way of the dogs, and is clearly a recent innovation following their arrival in the island. The rough platforms forming the beds proper were about fifty centimetres off the ground, but this distance varies from place to place – in the south, at Beniaboì I saw them about one metre off the ground, with the family fire under instead of beside them.

The beds are supported on four convenient branches forked at the top, on which the four poles forming the bed frame rest. The size of the frame varies between 1·55 × 0·65 metres and 1·15 × 0·43 metres, and on this small platform the entire family sleeps huddled together. The human members of the family lie longwise, all with their heads on the same log set as a head-rest (unless they are lucky enough to find a suitable giant bamboo washed up on the beach). Very occasionally a rush mat about half a metre square is laid on the platform, but usually the family just lies on bare canes packed tightly together on the frame parallel with the long side.

The hut at Tambe-e-buiè, its 1951 edition delayed till 1952 by the earthquake the previous year when part of the coast dropped, was rather larger than Toqué-è-bùie. In 1953 it was rebuilt twenty metres or so further back from the sea, but exactly as before. It has twelve beds, including two on the high platforms for the adolescents, one of which has two tiers, on the principle of our bunks. I saw this type of thing on a number of occasions and on one occasion I saw one being built out in the open, with the top platform three metres from the ground. All the beds at Tambe-e-buiè are rather higher than at Toqué-è-bùie (but not as high as Beniaboì) and were all arranged radially; the platform on which meat was kept was two metres off the ground.

An unusual feature of Tambe-e-buiè, which had a diameter of 13·55 metres and a maximum height of 4·5 metres, was a series of six vertical poles set in a straight line to support the main transverse beam, one of which could be regarded as a centre pole. The pole on each side of the centre formed part of the innermost circle of supporting poles; there were two more circles, all supporting rings of canes. Unusually, only one of the rings of canes supporting the roof did not rest on vertical poles. The outer ring was only 0·4 metres high and the edge of the roof almost touched the ground, although one could still brush the fronds apart and crawl out. The roof mats were rectangular, very well made, and larger than at Toqué-è-bùie; some were three and a half metres by three metres or more, laid over seven or ten split reeds, instead of the usual four or five.

No permanent hut, or even a temporary shelter, is ever built far from water supplies adequate for the number of people in the group. If there is none visible, the Onges know how to dig for it, providing not too much effort is required. The Semang and Aeta dig water-holes, and several authors have regarded the Andamanese as differing from them in this respect, but I am able to confirm that they can and do dig water-holes. I first saw them do so in 1951, and in 1952 and again in 1953, near Toqué-è-bùie, I was able to enlarge one. Originally it yielded very little water, and very dirty, as the Onges never bother to go further down than they must – a handful of water is enough. After I had enlarged the well it yielded over half a cubic metre an hour, and I had to build a fence round it to prevent the dogs wallowing in it. I gave the Onges buckets, rope, pick-axes and spades so they could get at clean water, although in view of their natural indolence I rather doubted whether they would be any use. In fact, they used the metal parts for arrow heads and went on as before, drinking out of foul pools covered in rotting vegetation and refuse. It is easy to have clear water on Little Andaman, naturally filtered over the coral formations and never more than two or three metres down, but the effort is too much for the Onges! Usually they drink like animals, lying flat on their stomachs with their lips to the water; some will fold a large leaf into a crude cup, however, and occasionally a fastidious individual will use a *Nautilus* shell.

The water-hole at Toqué-è-bùie alone, if properly maintained, would be able to supply enough water every day for at least five hundred people. The continual falling in of the sides, inevitable in a sandy area, could be permanently prevented by cementing them.

CHAPTER FOUR

A Journey into Prehistory

The complete lack of hygiene of the Onges does not explain their disturbing lack of fertility. Nor can filth, smoking or loose living fully explain the sterility of the surviving Arioto.

There must be some other cause, and this in all probability is merely biological. One might call it the senescence of a race brought about by their total isolation for thousands of years, exacerbated by being broken into small endogamous units, all mutually hostile. This is not the opinion of all (the few) who have studied the Andamanese, and the problem remains to be investigated further.

In the Onges at least it cannot be a question of malnutrition, as I had ample opportunity of seeing during my visits to the island. Food is abundant, both the land and the sea offer an inexhaustible supply, even to the point of sustaining life, alone, if necessary, to all the Andamanese. The Jarawas are the exception. Forced away from the sea into the forests, they are dependent on one source of food, and it is therefore possible to make some attempt to calculate the maximum number of people which could be supported by their territory. In the case of the Onges, however, living amid luxuriant vegetation, with a rich source of sea food nearby, a given area can support a far higher population, and the same is true of the Jarawas cut off on North Sentinel.

The food of the Jarawas consists mainly of pork, with fresh-water fish (including some excellent carp) river molluscs and crustacea in large quantities, roots, tubers, wild fruits and honey. The Arioto, staying as they did in the coastal areas of Great Andaman, must have lived mainly off the sea.

The small population reported in the Andamans by visitors to the islands in the middle of the last century cannot therefore be attributed to scarcity of food, nor can nutrition have had any effect on the demographic decadence. Strict endogamy over thousands of years, and fragmentation into smaller and smaller groups is perhaps a more likely explanation of the situation. The last stage has now been reached; the Arioto, for instance, who numbered six hundred and twenty-five in the 1901 census, had dwindled to twenty-three in 1955. In that year there were only two young children, a boy and a girl (of different parents) and the girl, about five years old, clearly had a Burmese father. The boy, however, named Sirake and then aged about eleven, intelligent and alert, with the very blue-black skin of the Andamanese and typical hair, may well be of pure stock. He is the only hope of continuing the ancient Arioto line, but this will be impossible unless a girl of pure stock is born shortly.

This seems unlikely. With the exception of these two couples, the Arioto appear to be sterile. I have myself seen their sorrow at being deprived of children, and one of them, named Moro, of fairly pure stock, told me of his grief. He took me to his wife, also of pure Andamanese origin, and externally as normal and healthy as her husband, but deserted by the spirits of fertility. Through no fault of their own, the cause probably lies in both of them.

In all the Andamanese, fertility seems always to have increased from the age of twenty-eight and to end by the age of forty-eight – in many cases thirty-eight, although since none of them know their age, owing to the absence of any form of counting, their deceptively youthful appearance makes assessment of age extremely difficult. I met only one woman who, as far as I could estimate, had borne seven children, and of these only three were still alive in 1954; the widespread custom by which children are transferred from one family to another, even during the period of lactation, to 'share' the enjoyment of them, made all the usual means of assessing the number of births virtually impossible. In a number of childless couples whom I saw on Little Andaman, the women are under twenty-eight and there is still hope of fertility, even if it is late. This could happen in the case of the wives of the two leaders Cocheggi and Cendubài; these two men married two sisters, among the healthiest and most beautiful women on the island, Vaghèghe and Tocuaghèghe, both under twenty-two. Neither of them has ever been pregnant, although both are apparently normal and enjoy the active marital relationships necessary, according to their husbands, to encourage the entry of the benevolent spirits which bring motherhood. The late onset of fertility in all Andamanese women and perhaps in men as well[1] probably depends on mechanisms which have been operating for a very long time, affecting the sex ratio at birth, and preferential infant mortality in one sex. By a combination of observation and deduction I was able to be reasonably certain that among the Onges at least more males are born than females. The disparity is reduced, though not eliminated, by a higher mortality rate in young males. Males thus remain in excess, making it difficult for some, possibly fertile, to find wives.

There are certain peoples – notably the Pitcairn Islanders – who have arisen by repeated inbreeding for hundreds of years from a very few individuals. It is clear from this example that genetic isolation and inbreeding cannot of themselves cause numerical, physical or mental decline of a population. The problem merits further investigation. Civilization has perhaps accused herself unjustly of causing the decline of primitive races, whereas she has in fact only hastened the disappearance of groups already heading for demographic decadence as the result of physiological factors which lie within the group itself, and which are consequently difficult to counteract. The intrinsic damage done by civilization as such has, in my opinion, been considerably exaggerated in some quarters.

Possibly because of the low birth rate the maternal instinct is very highly developed in the women of the Andamans, even to the point of 'adopting' children temporarily. These children are always given lavish affection, and are kept sometimes for years, or even permanently if the parents do not ask for them back. Given the language barrier, this custom makes census-taking difficult as childless couples happily declare adopted children as their own. Nabimbòi, with no children of her own, always had children with her, and it was only the fact that they differed from year to year that led me to suspect what was happening! One wonders whether the custom was not already common before outsiders first came to the Andamans, owing to the existence of a high incidence of sterility long before the arrival of civilization.

[1] There is some evidence of infertility in the men, but it is clear that this is of relatively minor importance.

The Onges are the most numerous of the three peoples surviving in the Andamans. Vigorous and apparently full of promise for the future they may well offer a suitable field for the application of eugenic measures designed to increase their numbers; this would be impossible with the Jarawas owing to their hostility towards outsiders, and the few remaining Arioto are nearly all of impure stock. If their confidence could be gained, it might be possible to encourage inter-marriage between the various groups, in the hope that fertility would increase and the ultimate total extinction of Onges, Jarawas and Arioto, would be prevented.

In the Andamanese, this physiological decline has been accompanied by cultural decadence, as my digs in the kitchen-middens all over the archipelago showed. The ancient pottery which came to light is proof enough; when one compares it with recent work the latter is indicative of secondary and not original primitiveness. The successive strata in the deposits show a gradual decline from earthenware clearly made from a very refined mix to crude ware with vegetable impurities and bits of stone left in the clay. The pots dating from ancient times were clearly well fired and the quality of the clay allowed them to have thin but nevertheless very strong walls. In the present-day ware, on the other hand, the wall has to be thick because of the coarseness of the clay, making the pots both heavy and easily broken. Moreover, firing is limited to drying the pots in the sun, and the clay is in fact only hardened when the pot is used for cooking.

Ignorance of fire-making in the Andamans may also stem from this cultural regression, as one of the effects of physiological and psychological decadence. Given the absence of magico-religious beliefs among the Andamanese, ignorance of fire-making cannot be attributed to any ritual taboo or veto. On the other hand, it is in sharp contrast to the possession of elements of cultural advance such as the bow, with highly developed arrows, the harpoon with its detachable point, and the outrigger canoe.

Few races are known, even in far distant times, which never had fire. *Sinanthropus* and nearly every fossil Man after him had fire, even if he was unable to create it and could only preserve it once received from some natural combustion. The Onges, while retaining a number of ethnic characteristics of the Palaeolithic era, have also acquired more recent additions, so that any primitive ignorance on their part of an art so ancient and generally advantageous as that of making fire is hardly credible. One thing is, however, certain: they do not today know how to produce fire.

In order to explain their ignorance, one must remember the surprising speed with which primitive peoples forget even essential facts, even details of their own life. They can forget their father's or mother's name, or both, and important events of less than fifty years ago are sometimes forgotten by those who took part in them. Cultural regression following the forgetting of ethnographical facts, even essential facts such as the making of fire, is a phenomenon widespread in every continent. Widely differing elements of culture spread out from a number of centres and were forced to adapt to natural surroundings often incomparably different from the centre from which they spread. Sometimes these cultural migrations led to progress, but more often to regression. Particularly in the marginal areas furthest from the centres of culture, enforced modifications were profound, with ensuing cultural impoverishment. The Andamanese, probably arriving from areas to the east, remain as survivors of a series of disasters both biological and non-biological, in one of the marginal areas which, although a natural paradise, has been most affected by adverse circumstances. It is, therefore, hardly surprising if, like the Eskimos, they no longer reflect the brilliance of the past, either biologically or culturally. A similar situation is to be found in populations much larger and more advanced than the Andamanese.

It is not strictly accurate to define the Onges as primitive; they should more properly be regarded as involuted. They possess certain essentials which almost entitle them to recognition as a civilized people: religious concepts are not unknown, they bury their dead, they are monogamous, and they have their own language. While they are unable to produce fire they can preserve it and know how to use it, they make excellent bows, arrows, harpoons and canoes, and they know how to produce pottery.

Nevertheless, they have no agriculture, and do not keep domestic animals except the dog, introduced only within living memory and to them a faithful friend. They have no idea of the use of metals, and make no stone implements apart from the tiny splinters used for shaving. They have never developed any graphic arts and have

1 The author with two adult islanders

3 *Above top* A group of Onges resting against the bastion roots of a
tree. The man in the centre is smoking a crab-claw pipe
4 *Above* A typical example of tight binding of the body as a cure for disease
2 *Left* Two examples of the geometric patterns which are painted on the
face and torso

5 *Above* Mother feeding her baby from a Nautilus shell
6 *Right* The axe is one of the few primitive tools in use in the Andamans

7 An important feature of the islands is the way in which the forest comes right down to the water's edge

8 In the monsoon season, trees are frequently uprooted in this manner

9 The bow and arrow is the main weapon used for hunting; in this photograph the archer has the long arrow harpoon used for spearing large fish

10 Fishing in the coral shallows

11 *Above* Launching an outrigger canoe
12 *Below* Hunter with a monitor lizard
13 Mother and child

14 In spite of their size, the Andaman islanders are capable of carrying
enormous weights

15 A temporary shelter in the forest

16 Making a roof section from palm fronds for a permanent dwelling

17 Completed permanent dwelling, which is also used for burial of the inhabitants

18 A family group with, on the right, the cylindrical cooking-pot, and the inevitable dogs

19 Typical shell collection from a kitchen-midden

only a crude form of body decoration based on geometrical designs.

They are, therefore, to be included among the most backward peoples of mankind, who have remained in a very simple form of social structure. They have never progressed to any elementary organization of themselves into 'clans', or even 'tribes'. They have, in short, the psychological outlook and concepts of other primitive peoples, modified by local conditions. The evidence in favour of the Onges of today being the product of cultural development over a very long period appears to me overwhelming, though their development has already been hindered by involution and, we must presume, a series of setbacks.

The Onges have thus remained culturally isolated and this has deprived them of the opportunities offered to the rest of the world. The time came when they ceased to receive or to elaborate new concepts, and from that point regression was inevitable. There is abundant evidence that their culture dates back to Palaeolithic times, so that they now represent the last and decadent expression of a very lengthy stage of biological and cultural development, a point of arrival, and not one of departure. Everywhere in the Andamans there are signs of an ancient culture which must once have spread over much of the world. It is neither logical nor practical to explain the similarity of many concepts as a series of convergences, all of independent origin; ideas must have spread outwards with the passage of time and the gradual population of habitable areas.

No study of present-day life on the Andamans can be complete without an attempt to build up a valid picture of the islands as they were centuries ago, and this we can do with some accuracy by a study of the kitchen-middens. These abound on Great Andaman, but few have been excavated, and then only briefly reported. Those of Little Andaman have not, for obvious reasons, previously been investigated, but they are of considerable importance for the light they cast on their own development and history, and on that of similar mounds outside the Andamans. It is only on Little Andaman that they are still being built up, continually increasing in size, forming a unique, direct and continuous link with life on the island thousands of years ago.

Provided they have not been damaged – for example by rain or earth tremors – they are all regular in shape. The base is circular, and the round mound rises as a truncated cone, at an angle of forty-five degrees. The circumference at the base varies, and can be as small as fifty metres, although a hundred and twenty to a hundred and fifty metres is more usual, and some are even larger. The height of the cone varies from two to ten metres or more, depending on the length of time the site has been in continuous occupation.

Excavations showed how slowly these mounds have accumulated, often only twenty centimetres in a hundred years. This is due to pressing down of the mound by the normal activities of the occupants of the hut, and by the fact that the Onges move so frequently from place to place; only about a sixth of the year is spent in the communal huts. It is possible that over the undisturbed centuries before outsiders came to the island the middens grew rapidly, but it is not unreasonable to assume a growth of ten metres in five thousand years. Dating by the radio-carbon method, which it is hoped is to be undertaken at the University of Rome, should confirm this estimate.

Before I began digging I had, although with some reservations, accepted the standard ideas about the formation of the kitchen-middens. I was, for example, doubtful about their regular shape, which did not seem to fit the accepted theory that those of Great Andaman were related to purely temporary encampments; I did not see that the very regular shape of the middens fitted such a picture.

On Great Andaman, the continuous strife between Arioto and Eremtaga, making permanent camps too vulnerable, led to their final disappearance at the beginning of the century and all further growth of the middens ceased. Most of them are in the coastal areas, and must therefore derive from the Arioto. Previous investigators were therefore handicapped by having to excavate abandoned mounds, of which none of the islanders had any personal knowledge and which they could not attempt to explain.

It seemed, therefore, that to gain any real knowledge of these structures, and hence of the people both past and present who built them up, it would be necessary to dig in the active mounds of Little Andaman. These derived from the communal huts on the island which interested me particularly – Cemalè, Lulera, Torabeh and Totamaddulù, the first a day's journey into the forest from Berié-Abdalù, the second two days from Labanar, and the others both near Togalanghe.

On both Great Andaman and Little Andaman the kitchen-middens yield a vast quantity of animal remains, bones and a great number of shells, with very little earth. The shells diminish in the upper levels, to be replaced by bones of *Sus andamanensis*, the wild pig of the islands, the change coinciding with the arrival of the dog in the islands; the revolution which this introduction brought into the life of the islanders is at once evident.

My first excavations in 1951 were limited to establishing which mounds looked promising for future digs. I made soundings in the north, middle and south of Great Andaman and found that near each midden there were invariably abundant food supplies, as well as fresh water, sometimes running, sometimes in pools. The excavations went on for sixty days, aided by a first-class gang of men from Bihar, who even agreed, in view of the necessity of concentrated digging, to forgo their customary feast days. To these preliminary excavations I returned later on a number of occasions,[1] using them as controls.

My first real dig began on 5 January 1952 in a fine midden on Middle Andaman, a few hours' march from the forest station of Long Island, at a place known as Beehive Hill, or Golpahar in Hindi. The water pipe installed for the benefit of the colonists on Long Island draws from a spring, and on its way to the reservoir on the shore it runs right through the centre of the midden. Emerging, it runs for a hundred and fifty metres through a mangrove swamp stinking with vile black mud, which in fact served as an excellent means of dating the layers, by relating them to the rise and fall in the ground level of the swamp over the last few thousands of years.

The whole of the time we were there we had to work with look-outs posted ready for any Jarawas trying an ambush; to the north of the midden the grave of a Burmese killed by them a short time before was a grim warning. We did a great deal of shooting, but fortunately only for game. Fallow deer descended from imported

[1] With a number of young Indians very kindly allocated to my assistance by the anthropological service of the Government of India, and to all of whom I am greatly indebted for their enthusiastic help, often under the most trying conditions.

beasts were plentiful, and used to come right up to the camp out of curiosity, in spite of the noise of the shooting, and my men took so many that they were able to dry and smoke some for future use. There were flocks of pigeons after the fruit in the *Ficus* trees, and another rather smaller bird with green wings (*àriel* in Hindi). There were always large fish lying quietly on the surface of the sea, only two hundred metres from the dig, so that we could shoot these as well. The Jarawas were kept at bay, we all fed very well, and everyone was highly satisfied!

The camp was surrounded night and day by a chorus of frogs, and the lights of the camp attracted a whole army of hermit crabs; in the dry season they made an incredible noise parading up and down the dry leaves, even rummaging round our beds inside the tents while we were trying to get to sleep. They disappeared, suddenly and completely, immediately the rains came. Like the rest of their species they use their claws to close the shells in which they have made their home. Usually the large claw was able to do the job alone, but in case of difficulty they would bring the other claw and even their legs into the battle, until they managed to close the shell completely (my men enjoyed these struggles immensely). They in fact use various shells, and squeeze into them somehow, even into the cowries. Some varieties use nothing but cowries and their claws and legs have become very slender in adapting themselves to the narrow shell.

Unlike the hermit crabs, the rats were not affected by the seasons and came after our stores in hordes. I collected a number of species, but I was never able to catch one kind which particularly interested me. It was a jumping variety, graceful and rather larger than our mouse, with big ears, and a very pointed muzzle. The front feet were short, almost atrophied, and the back ones long, with strong, powerfully muscled haunches, so that the creature was rather like the rats of the pyramids in miniature. I often surprised them round my tent if I shone a torch suddenly, but they would bound away out of reach on their hind legs and no traps seemed to attract them. This variety does not seem to have been reported, at least in the Andamans, and it was the only one I was never able to catch.

When the rains came the disappearance of the hermit crabs was matched by the equally sudden appearance of curious cicadas, which chirped intermittently like all those in the Andamans. By the end of June 1953 there were legions of them. In contrast to the frogs, who were completely silent unless the atmosphere was calm, these cicadas only chirped when it was pouring with rain and blowing a gale, and then only at dawn and at dusk. Unlike other Asiatic species, they hopped from tree to tree between their momentary bursts of chirping, so that from minute to minute the chirping moved en bloc and made it almost impossible to catch them. When they were silent they were completely invisible against the branches, so that although we knew they were motionless we were still unable to catch them.

Surrounded by these diversions we began digging seriously. I must make it clear from the outset that in recording my findings I make no claim to saying the last word on the subject. All I hope to do is to report what I have been able to deduce from the combination of my personal observations of islanders as they are today and the evidence which I found in their kitchen-middens both of the past and of the present.

Though not as large as some I found later, the midden at Golpahar, like all the rest, was a truncated cone, beaten into a dome by the monsoons, and at the time of my excavation it was about five metres high with a circumference of a hundred and ten metres and a diameter of thirty-six metres. I removed half, leaving the other half so that others might later check my findings.

Ninety per cent of the contents proved to be shells, chiefly bi-valves, and mainly *Cyrena*. As the shell content was clearly fairly constant I tried to calculate the total in the whole midden; and by taking into account the nomadic life of the present-day inhabitants of the island, and their eating habits, it was possible to reach a reasonable estimate of the age of the deposit.

Each midden can be regarded as attributable to the food refuse of groups of thirty to forty people, living at the site for forty to fifty days a year or less. Shellfish can never have been the islanders' sole diet. They are certainly not today – shellfish of any kind are only eaten when there is nothing else to be had, and then only in certain localities where it is not too much trouble to carry them to the camp. In other words, although shells formed the greater part of the deposit, they will only have been added to it sporadically. In the absence of some complete change of habits, unlikely in such cautious people as the Andamanese, we may deduce that the midden rose extremely slowly, taking four to five thousand years to reach its present size. One also has to take into account periods of complete abandonment, evidenced by sterile layers of black mud, resulting from changes in the level of the nearby swamps, so that very great antiquity of the midden can be confidently assumed.

The Golpahar midden, however, does not date from the first arrival of the Negritos in the archipelago. Another nearby, with a circumference at the base of little over fifty metres, and three metres high, has in its lowest layers abundant remains of bivalves which are now rare if not absent in the Andamans, and completely absent at Golpahar itself. Among them are *Ostrea crista galli* and *Pectunculus aurantius*. The close proximity of the two middens may indicate the abandonment of the smaller for a new and larger site. Future investigations will show whether the smaller of these two is in fact the oldest attributable to the Negritos; it is the same type as that at Maya Bandar, where appalling weather and mud forced me to abandon work.

To establish comparisons between enough middens to draw any real conclusions as to their antiquity and the date of Man's arrival in the archipelago, it will be necessary to excavate and map a large number. At the moment, apart from the few previous excavations to which I have referred, mine are the only ones and I cannot overstress the necessity for further work to establish, or refute, the tentative conclusions I have drawn.

On Little Andaman food of all kinds is so abundant that shells were comparatively rare among the refuse, and the middens have grown much more slowly. It is, moreover, difficult to identify the abandoned ones, as the luxuriant vegetation hides them from view. It is not impossible, however, that they may ultimately be shown to date further back than those on Great Andaman, and that this, together with the fact of their continued growth at the present time, may provide valuable information.

At Golpahar, apart from the shells forming ninety per cent of the lower strata, I found bones of marine and land mammals, and of fish, turtles and birds, arrow heads made of bone, *Tridacna* and the spines of large fish, bits of stone, and an enormous number of tiny splinters of obsidian and other very hard materials.

In some places it was difficult to identify the various layers. Normal palaeontological criteria were difficult to apply, as most of the remains belonged to species still extant. Some chronological assistance was given, however, by four different stratifications due to evident changes in the level of the adjacent marshes, resulting not from any general marine phenomena, but from numerous land movements. On these occasions the cliffs sank, the sea flowed inland and corals flourished, later to be buried by the black ooze and mud of the mangrove swamps.

The maximum rise in the sea-level during the growth of the midden was a little over three metres, and affected a wide area. The date could be established by a full geological study of the archipelago as a whole, but it is clear that although this and similar occurrences had direct stratigraphic effects on the middens, the results were manifest only over very long periods of time.

Refuse from introductions of European origin, such as pipes, glass bottles, shot pellets, pieces of iron, etc., appear in the top level, only fifteen centimetres thick and dating back about a hundred years. There were no dog bones either here or anywhere else on Little or Great Andaman. Recently introduced, the dog clearly caused an increase in the amount of pig remains, and a parallel reduction in shell refuse. Below the fifteen centimetres level, iron, imported pipes and glass fragments disappear, and the crab-claw pipes, still used today by the Onges, begin to emerge. The smoking habit must, as I have said, date from very ancient times, as traces of these claw pipes appear in the lowest strata, in contact with virgin soil.[1]

The actual consistency of the layers, which vary considerably, can tell us much. At Golpahar, we reached a depth of about four metres from the top of the midden through refuse mixed with only a little loose earth, very easy to penetrate. Bones, shells and other objects emerged clean, as if only recently rejected. The situation altered suddenly about one metre from the bottom, when the strata became hard and cemented with a mixture of ashes and earth. In these layers the shells were calcified by exposure to fire, and so fragile that they could only be recovered in broken pieces.

[1] It is obvious that smoking is a very ancient vice; leaves of the wild hemp are still smoked in Africa as they were long before the discovery of tobacco and claw pipes like those of the Onges are found in Eastern New Guinea, especially on the south coast, and as far as the Torres Straits and the Melville Straits. In Australia these pipes appear only in a few coastal areas in the east and north, including the Gulf of Carpentaria, and they are not found in the rest of Australia or in Polynesia.

It is clear from this that when they first arrived in the Andamans, the Negritos had no pottery; there are no signs of it at all in the lowest levels. Before they acquired the use of earthenware, perhaps for centuries, they baked their shellfish in ashes, so that the shells became calcified; but as time went on they came to boil them, as the islanders still do today. There is a clear distinction between the ashy, fragile, almost fossilized appearance of the former, and the cleaner solidity of the latter.

In the lowest level in which it appears, the pottery shows signs of careful working of the clay and good firing, degenerating towards more recent times. The uppermost layers reveal the crudest ware, the clay being impure, carelessly mixed, with bits of stone in it and hardly fired at all; it appears to have been merely dried by exposure to the sun and hardened in the course of normal use, as the Onges do today. The resulting pots break easily, despite their thickness, in contrast to the thinner, but much stronger, walls of earlier pottery. They were built up by the coil technique, exactly as they are made on Chowra, the one island in the Nicobars which specializes in pottery.

On Great Nicobar, among the Shom-Pen, these exists also another, cruder type of pottery which is made by a very primitive method. A basket is covered with clay, and hardened in the fire without being properly fired; fragments of this type of pottery retain the marks of the basket inside. The kitchen-middens of the Andamans contain no traces of any primitive stage of this kind; instead, a somewhat refined form of earthenware appears suddenly. There are traces of ornamentation, rows of small lines, usually roughly parallel. No such ornamentation appears on the crude ware of more recent date, however.

Andamanese pots have always been made with a pointed base which prevents their standing upright, so that they have to be carried in baskets, exactly like those of the Shom-Pen, who make their pots in complete ignorance of the Andamanese and Chowra pottery.

Pottery did not form part of the culture of the Negritos of ancient times. Neither the Semang of Malacca nor the Aetà of the Philippines, their last remnants, nor the Andamanese, had any. The custom of hollowing out logs for use as vessels, and the continuing use of the earth oven, doubtless made the absence of any pottery no hardship.

If we may deduce from the evidence of the middens, pottery arrived in the Andamans at the same time as the pig, bones of which appear only in the upper levels; but we know nothing of the people responsible for the introduction of either. It is, however, certain that both arrived in Great Andaman and Little Andaman together.

There are indications that Little Andaman was the first to feel the benefit of pottery, possibly introduced by a light-skinned people. There are, as I have said, significant variations of skin colour and stature among the Onges; some have markedly lighter skins than the other islanders, and one would assume that this feature entered Little Andaman from the Nicobars with the unknown people who brought with them pottery and the pig. The people as an entity have disappeared as a result of inter-marriage with the indigenous population, while pigs reverted to the wild state and flourished, even spreading from one island to another by swimming (I can vouch for this, having seen them do it).[1]

The indications are that there were migrations from Little Andaman to Great Andaman long before those from which the Jarawas derive. In certain respects they resemble the Onges, whereas the surviving Arioto appear to represent a purer stock. The Onges seem to have acquired foreign blood in relatively recent times, perhaps when pigs and pottery appeared, when the kitchen-middens of Great Andaman were already being built up by the Arioto, but before the migration northwards by which the Jarawas reached their present home. Much more intensive investigation of the middens will, however, be needed before these hypotheses can be confirmed.

At Golpahar there were within the midden five graves containing human bones, not in anatomical position, and clearly filled in with fresh earth. I was surprised to find only the long bones, skulls and jawbones; the remaining bones could not be found. This may be explained by the custom among the Arioto (still prevailing

[1] One thing is puzzling: the three remaining groups of primitive Negritos in Malacca and the Philippines have the arrow harpoon with a detachable head. This is particularly valuable in the forests against the pigs, which cannot escape into the undergrowth once they have been hit. But it is difficult to see how or why the arrow harpoon reached the Andamans, where there were at that time no large mammals. It seems necessary to postulate the former spread of the weapon with the Negritos over a very wide area and its use against a much wider range of animals.

among the Onges) of wearing not only necklaces of the carpals and tarsals of deceased kin or pieces of rib, but also, in some groups, the skulls, painted with ochre and hanging from a cord round the neck. The long bones, painted red and white, were reburied in the communal hut. The Onges of today carry only the coloured jaw-bones of their kin.

No ornaments were found in the middens, nor did we expect to find any, as at death the Onges (and presumably their ancestors) bury all the personal objects of the deceased secretly in the forest, where the termites destroy all traces.

Not all the Arioto can have carried skulls and jawbones. Some clearly carried neither, as all the bones are sometimes found in the middens. A few middens are completely without human bones, particularly in the Port Blair area. Nevertheless at Ciauldari (or Chowldary), ten kilometres to the west, I found in January 1954 long bones without the skull or jawbones, and at Maya Bandar in 1953 I saw almost complete skeletons, not in anatomical posi-tion, owing to exhumation and reburial, but including skull, jaw-bones and in a number of cases the small bones as well.

The evidence of the middens thus clearly shows that burial and subsequent customs differed considerably among the various groups of islanders in the past, as they do today. The majority, judging from the Onges, seem to have remained faithful to a given custom, the dead in all cases continuing to remain a part of the group, whether or not any particular bone was carried about by the members of the group.

It is somewhat surprising to find customs varying so markedly in so primitive and numerically small a population, even though isolated in groups. The explanation lies in the fact that long-esta-blished customs may be altered overnight as the result of a 'revela-tion' by some seer, only to have the new customs overthrown themselves in the course of time by the next 'revelation'. I had an experience of this in the Onges when Enagaghe, a well-known seer, announced one day that he had received an order from the spirits about the way in which hunting trophies were to be displayed. No longer were pig jawbones to be impaled one behind the other on poles hung horizontally along the sloping roof of the hut a little above the hunter's bed. The whole skull, including the jaw-bones, was to be preserved, the bones held together in their natural position by reed cords, which were to be tied in front of the snout, ending in a cord by which the skull was to be hung above the hunter's bed. No sooner said than done, and at the beginning of 1954 all the old trophies were thrown out into the forest, to be gradually replaced by the new ones. Fortunately I had collected some of the old trophies before the 'revelation'!

From the evidence of the middens it would appear that these variations in burial customs have no practical basis, and probably all derive from similar 'revelations'. Further investigations in a large series of the deposits, enabling dated comparisons to be made, would be extremely revealing.

Even allowing for these sudden alterations in established customs, it is clear that their elaboration indicates slow and hardly perceptible development over long periods of time and the middens must be dated in millennia. The hypothesis put forward by some scholars that the Andamanese are descended from negro slaves who escaped while on their way to the Portuguese colonies in India in the sixteenth or, at the earliest, fifteenth centuries, seems therefore quite untenable, in face of the abundant evidence in favour of the great antiquity of the middens and of the people who built them up.

It seems clear that during the last few thousand years, successive waves of migration have taken place over a whole area bounded on the west by the Andamans and Nicobars. All indications point to a close connection between the Andamanese and the peoples to the westward, the Negrito element remaining alone and almost untouched in the Andamans, but becoming submerged in the Nicobars into the mongoloid element of more recent origin. Even today a number of Nicobarese show signs of Negrito ancestry; short in stature, they have crinkly hair which although long is very different from the straight black hair of the mongoloid element, and their heads, noses and lips bear clear signs of Negrito ancestry.

In addition to these more general conclusions the middens also cast some light on the origin, still somewhat problematical, of the wretched Jarawas of Great Andaman. Comparisons between their middens and those of the Onges show that there were in the past communal huts on Great Andaman exactly the same as those still extant today on Little Andaman.

The continual fighting between the Eremtaga and the Arioto led, as we have seen, to the gradual disappearance of the communal huts of the latter as being too vulnerable. Subsequently, the conflict still going on between foreigners and Jarawas completed the destruction, so that there are now no communal huts on Great Andaman. The ever-increasing violence of the punitive expeditions against the Jarawas put an end to their numerical recovery during the last fifteen years or so, and there may indeed now be none left. Today only their kitchen-middens, and the surviving Onges, remain to show us how the Jarawas must have lived.

The Jarawa middens are distinguishable from those of the Arioto by their inland position and by their content of freshwater shellfish and land gasteropods, not eaten by the peoples of the coast.

Like the kitchen-middens of the Onges, those of the Jarawas contain human bones clearly interred in graves, and not scattered among the refuse. This refutes the Arioto accusation against the Eremtaga of cannibalism, and that of the people of South Andaman (now vanished) against the people of North Andaman and the Onges; the remains of cannibal feasts would undoubtedly have been found among kitchen refuse and not carefully buried in the ritual manner, with the graves filled in with earth. And the Jarawas and the majority of the Arioto buried their dead in the communal huts, continuing a custom which originated while they were still on Little Andaman. In time variations arose, but this does not alter the evidence in favour of migration in ancient times from the south, via the Nicobars and Little Andaman.

The differences in culture between the islands can be explained by the ease with which primitive peoples forget. The Jarawas, for example, although they reached Great Andaman by sea from Little Andaman, forgot in a few generations the art of hollowing canoes when they were forced to live in the depths of the forests, far from the sea. Today, they have been free from the Arioto for some time, at least on the west coast, and have access to the sea, but they have not started building canoes again. In other things, however, such as burial rites, the Jarawas kept faithful to the old Onge customs; their middens show the same exhumation of the bones, the same cleaning, and tinting with ochre, and careful reburial.

The general similarity of the middens in Great and Little Andaman cannot be due to chance. Animal food, for example, has clearly been cooked in the same way; the bones are never charred, but always have the appearance of being cooked in an earth oven. The direct roasting of large game over the fire, postulated by some authorities, including Brown, was never practised; the islanders preferred to go on as they had done since time immemorial, because it was more efficient – witness the traces of the earth oven which are to be found all over the world, including Europe. In Polynesia and Micronesia, and among the pygmies of Asia and Africa, it was widely used; variations when they arose did so as the result of local circumstances, like that of throwing water on the fire instead of using fleshy leaves, when there were none in the area. But the basic principle remained the same everywhere, and the use of the earth oven coincides with the geographical distribution of hunting, gathering and burial customs similar to those found in the Andamans.

In April 1954 I excavated the midden at Tambe-e-buiè on Little Andaman, abandoned after the earth tremors of 1951, to investigate the position of the beds. The custom of burying the dead underneath their beds made it possible to trace the latter by the human remains below them, arranged in a circle round the periphery. The Onges themselves helped in the work, sometimes even trying to recognize the remains as they came to light.[1] There were clear signs of reburial. The body is buried immediately after death at least one metre deep; whereas after exhumation, cleaning and colouring, it is never re-interred more than thirty centimetres below the floor of the hut. When another death makes it necessary for a new grave to be dug under the bed, the piles of bones from the second are disturbed, so that in time a form of ossuary develops. In this it is not possible to identify the various remains of individuals unless some change in the position of the hut, even by a few metres, preserves the bones from disturbance by fresh graves. Traces of the graves always remain, however, as they are invariably filled with fresh earth.

We have already seen that on Little Andaman the introduction of the dog reduced the consumption of shellfish (and hence the rate

[1] The material recovered is now in the Anthropological Museum of the Andamans and Nicobars, which I helped to establish at Port Blair. The museum was inaugurated on 6 June 1953 in the presence of the Governor, Mr A. K. Ghosh and the chief Indian officials of the town.

of growth of the kitchen-middens), judging by the number of shells in the deposits. On Great Andaman, on the other hand, the Jarawas, unable to keep dogs for fear of revealing their whereabouts with the barking, continued as they had always done, and the gradual disappearance of their middens was due not to any change in eating habits but to the breakdown of the communal hut system. Among the Arioto, already decimated for over a century by fighting with the Eremtaga, the dog seems to have had no effect on the situation, as the Arioto had dogs as far back as 1857. Possibly they regarded them in the same way as the Onges who, though deeply attached to them and quite incapable of eating them at any time, never go so far as to bury their bones in the middens; the carcase is thrown out into the forests for the monitors and the termites to dispose of. It is also probable that the introduction of the dog came too late, when the Arioto were already too depleted numerically for any change in their eating habits to be appreciably reflected in their middens.

In both Great and Little Andaman the middens are found only where the communal huts have been constantly rebuilt on the same sites. Where the ground permits, the base circle (or rarely, the ellipse) has been moved somewhat from side to side, without, however, greatly affecting the regularity of the shape. At Totamaddalù on Little Andaman I was interested to see that although the diameter of the midden lessened as the numbers of the group occupying the hut dwindled, the site remained unchanged. Today the base area of the midden is very extensive compared with the size of the hut now built on it, but its anthropological value is thereby increased.

The advent of the dog into the archipelago in about 1857 vastly increased the amount of meat available to the Andamanese. Once introduced into Little Andaman[1] the dog population increased explosively, as the Onges dare not kill any of the pups; the women even go so far as to suckle motherless pups themselves. This inordinate love of dogs has allowed the animals to become a pest. They already considerably outnumber the human population; families of only three or four people may have ten or twelve dogs,

[1] The dog reached Little Andaman only at the beginning of the present century; von Eichstedt in 1928 noted that the Onges had very few of them.

often extremely vicious but good hunters. The dogs often roam the forests in packs, hunting and devouring young pigs. The Onges will do nothing about it unless someone forces them to, but if this pack hunting is not stopped the pig will become extinct in ten or twenty years and in 1954 I tried myself (in vain) to draw the attention of the authorities to the situation.

The dog appears in even the most ancient of cultures in Australia, but did not spread to Tasmania, despite the geographical proximity. It arrived on Great Andaman with the establishment of the Indian penal colony and it is thus the Indian pariah which ultimately populated the whole archipelago. A despised outcast in India, the pariah became in the Andamans of enormous value, reverting to its ancient hunting instincts. Burmese police officials taught the islanders how to use the animal for hunting and within a few years it had revolutionized their methods. It led the islanders in fact, to comparative indolence; the dog worked for them, supplying with far less effort as much game as they used to catch in their long, weary and not always successful expeditions. Dogs meant invariable and abundant success in the hunt, and it is hardly surprising that the Andamanese came to develop a somewhat unbalanced affection for them.

On Little Andaman the dogs, with abundant food supplies always easily available, became physically far superior to their ancestors in India; unlike the pariahs they were well muscled, with good skins and coats, although most of them bear the marks of old and recent gashes by boar tusks.

On Great Andaman the dogs voluntarily catch and kill fallow deer. These, like the dogs, have increased to the extent of becoming a pest. The Arioto and Jarawas will not eat them for superstitious reasons, and so they have bred like wildfire, spreading to all the islands as far as Rutland. They swim well, but only with land in sight, and the greater distances involved have so far prevented them from spreading to Little Andaman.

Here the dogs have only one main prey – the pigs. Unlike the deer with their slender legs they cannot outdistance the dogs, and their only defence is to hide under the buttresses of the tree-trunks. The pig rushes underneath the tree, and faces the dogs like a stag at bay. There is no escape, only a few more terrible minutes of life. The pig fights the dogs off desperately, the males inflicting serious gashes with their tusks, unaware of the spear thrower coming up from behind. The result is inevitable. The dangerous boars are killed outright, but whenever possible the pig is, like the turtles, trussed helplessly and vivisected, again strictly according to established ritual, and again with an unconscious cruelty that is to Western eyes unbelievable. The liver, lungs, heart and intestines are the dogs' reward, and in a matter of minutes they are gone and the last drop of blood licked up.

Before every hunt the dogs are left hungry, on the principle that a well-fed dog does not hunt. If a young or small pig is caught by the pack during the hunt the Onges at once drag the body away and lodge it in the fork of a bush or tree. I have also seen this done if a full-grown pig is caught which is too thin, or unhealthy, or if a sow is taken, as the Onges find the females less tasty. In the dry season, when food is scarce and the pigs are less aggressive, they can be caught by one dog alone.

In the rainy season pork is, to the Onge palate, at its best. The pigs are fat and tasty, gorging on the lush vegetation that follows the onset of the south-west monsoon till they become slow, and easy prey. The dogs follow their tracks easily on the sodden ground, and the usual orgy of slaughter follows day after day, the Onges caring little for tomorrow and nothing for the day after. It is only owing to the fall in the numbers of the human population that the pig is still extant on the island; in compensation for the continuous slaughter I saw whole areas of forest round deserted communal huts where the earth had been literally ploughed up by the snouts of innumerable pigs rooting undisturbed for tubers.

During the hunt a number of dogs inevitably lose themselves in the maze of vegetation, and are cut off from the pack. Usually they manage to find their way back to one of the camps. When I went on long journeys into the forest we were always followed by strays. Greeting each other as though they were old friends they would quickly join the pack we used to take with us to hunt for the party. A stray will always try to find its own master, and any that are left behind during the hunt howl desperately like jackals. Others join in, in an eerie chorus, pausing every now and again as though waiting for their master's reply. Their howling is a curious reversion to the wild state – all the canines fear solitude, wherever

they may be, and the strays of the Andaman forests howl unceasingly. Even in the Onge encampments the dogs howl enough to
wake their sleeping masters; the only way to stop the noise is for
the Onges to forestall it by taking their dogs into the family bed,
fleas and all. There ensues silence, warmth and more fleas!

Hunting weapons of the Andamanese, the Semang and the Aetà
were originally made by all three peoples in a similar way, common
to all the Negritos. None have any defensive weapons as such;
their bows and arrows, never feathered, serve as arms as well as
for hunting and fishing. Shields are unknown and spears, rare in
the Andamans and among the Semang, are apparently no longer
in use among the Aetà; where they exist they are usually mainly
for hunting. All three peoples, however, have the arrow harpoon.[1]

Their bows are all clearly derived from the same source. In the
Andamans, only the Onges and Jarawas have remained true to the
original form, local variations arising at a later date, and they afford
additional evidence in favour of Little Andaman being the original
springboard from which the Negritos entered Great Andaman.

All the Negritos make their bows from one piece of wood stripped longitudinally from the living trunks of large trees such as
Mimusops littoralis or *Pterocarpus dalbergoides*. After they have been
left to season the strips are patiently fashioned into the required
shape; for this the Onges use the shells of *Cyrena* (the freshwater
species, which are tougher). The bows are straight, thicker in the
middle and gradually tapering towards the ends, and are usually
1·6 metres long, although there are exceptions. The cross section
is the same throughout the length of the bow, varying from three
or four centimetres diameter at the centre to two and a half centimetres at the horns. The inner surface is so slightly curved as to be
almost flat, while the back is markedly convex. The blunt horns
end in a 'shoulder and neck' stop to take the string, the neck
projecting about one and a half centimetres beyond the shoulders
– enough to hold the bowstring. The shoulder is formed by strips
of *Ficus* bark wound round the bow, or the yellow fibres of *Dendro-
bium*; one shoulder is invariably larger than the other. The string
itself, made from long thin strips of *Ficus* bark twisted together,
has a very narrow loop on one end and a larger one at the other;

[1] See p. 86.

when stretched the string remains held in place by the two loops, one too small to slip over the lower shoulder, and the larger one held firm on the upper shoulder by the tension of the string.

When the bow is strung, it is placed upright with the lower horn firmly on the ground, the string already looped on to the small shoulder. The top of the bow is forced down (either hand being used indiscriminately), a foot being pressed against the grip to help it bend; the other end of the string, with the large loop, is then run up the stave and slipped over the larger shoulder, where the tension holds it firm. Considerable individual variation may occur in the art of making the bow and preparing the string and also in the actual stringing. In the Onges, apart from the size of the bow, the variation never went beyond slight differences in the curvature of the inner surface and back, the former being in a few cases quite flat, or even concave, as in the Jarawa bows. Neither the Onges nor the Jarawas, including those on North Sentinel, decorate their bows in any way, but the Arioto like to make a series of small straight cuts on the horns, on both the inner and outer surfaces and sometimes even cover the bow with bizarre red and white lines, which wear off very quickly with use. There appears to be no real difference between Onge and Jarawa bows, except that the latter tend to be larger, in keeping with their intended use as hostile weapons.

From the original Negrito bow of Little Andaman the so-called S-bow of the Arioto evolved as the result of a number of minor innovations. The basic principle remained the same, but in an effort to take greater advantage of the elasticity of the wood the rudiments of the distinction between the two horns later developed into a distinction between the two halves of the bow.

The unique modification which the original form of bow underwent on Great Andaman turned the stave into a composite of two spear-shaped halves, the upper almost straight, the lower slightly curved. At the horns the bow is still almost round in section, flattening as the 'spear' broadens out; the general dimensions and shape of the bow vary little between the Arioto of the south and north of the island, although the latter make the diameter at the horns rather larger. The two halves are joined at the centre of the weapon, forming a grip which is the thickest part of the bow. The simple difference in the size of the shoulders in the Onge bow now becomes more complex; the upper horn is more pointed than the lower, and there is a difference between the upper and lower halves of the bow, as it is necessary to prevent the loops of the strings slipping on the bow. The bow string is made not from *Ficus* bark, as in the Onge bow, but from thin *Anadendron* fibres, twisted together and waxed with beeswax; it has the usual loop at each end, and the bow is strung with the help of the foot as in the simpler version. When strung, this type of bow becomes S-shaped as a result of the variations in elasticity arising from the spear-shape of the two halves, but when drawn it assumes the normal shape. The fact that it is easier to draw an S-bow than a single-curve one, without any loss of propulsive force, is an interesting mechanical point.

The bows are only strung when required for use, and in the normal way neither they nor the arrows are ever seen by outsiders; they disappear up into the roof of the communal hut, or into the bushes round the temporary camps. Even with friendly Onges I had to ask specifically to see them, or surprise their owners out hunting.

The external influences to which the Semang and Aetà have been subjected have been strong enough to make them to a large extent forget their original form of bow, which has however survived alongside a large number of cultural inovations. The differences, for example, between the upper and lower extremities of both bow and string have persisted, and the shoulder-and-neck stop (although this is now made by notching the bow-stave deeply) so that we may reasonably assume that a close study of the Onge bow will give us the essential characteristic of a very ancient form of the weapon. The greatest modification to the original form is the one which has been made on North Andaman, and in an attempt to improve the effect of separate curving of the two sections selected trees are deliberately trained for the purpose, the cut wood being seasoned slowly over heat and smoke, paying particular care to the parts which will take the greatest strain. As a result the 'give' in the bow is markedly increased. But even here no fundamental alteration has been made in the design of the weapon.

The Onge bow, therefore, represents the forerunner of the somewhat more highly evolved type (now dying out with their owners) on Great Andaman, and adds further support to the evidence for the arrival of the Negritos in the Andamans from the south; yet more evidence is provided by the Onge arrows. In the Andamans there are two types of arrows, those used for fish, and those for game, the latter also being used against human targets.

The same arrows are found throughout the archipelago, confirming a common origin. Only the dimensions vary from one area to another and that only very slightly; the Onges have both the biggest fishing arrows, and the biggest arrow harpoons, and the Arioto the smallest. In the past the islanders used arrows with from two to four points for fish, but I was unable to find any traces of them; those picked up on North Sentinel some years ago were possibly the last to be made.

The fishing arrow of the Andamans is made basically from the small native bamboo. The Onges remove the knots by scraping them down gradually with *Cyrena* shells, and then cut off a length varying between seventy centimetres and about one metre. Into one end they fix securely a hardwood stick, fifteen to twenty centimetres long. This foreshaft takes the head, now nearly always iron, but in the past made of wood, fish spines or pig bone. In the kitchen-middens I also found heads made out of shaped pieces of *Tridacna*. The three parts of the arrow are then bound together with very thin waxed fibres, wound carefully round and round, great care being taken to prevent the bamboo shaft splitting where the foreshaft is forced in. The completed arrow finishes up 1–1·15 metres long overall. The head is barbed, to hold the fish once it is hit; to get it out the whole arrow has to be pulled through. Sometimes, but not always, the shaft has a notch in it, to take the cord, care being taken to make the notch never more than two centimetres from any knot, to avoid any possibility of the shaft splitting. Alternatively, splits are prevented by binding waxed thread tightly round the shaft.

The hunting arrow, or arrow harpoon, is an intelligent adaptation, the result of acute observation of wild life, and is more complicated than the fishing arrow which is intended only to pierce the victim. The hunting arrow must not only score a hit, it must also prevent the animal from escaping into the undergrowth and force it to reveal its position. The harpoon holds the victim cruelly and securely, and the excruciating pain caused by the drag of the cord forces the animal to reveal its position by its cries of agony. The screams of a wild boar can be heard for hundreds of metres, draw-ing the hunters in from all sides, eager to take it alive. If it proves to be a large male, whose tusks can inflict appalling injuries, the hunters kill it at once with a spear or with a third type of arrow which has a long fixed head. This type of arrow, which does not differ greatly from those found in other parts of the world, is still used by some of the Andamanese against human enemies.

The shaft of the arrow harpoon is made preferably from *Tetran-thera lancifolia*, very common all over the archipelago. The wood for the shafts has to be straight, very slender at one end, where a notch is cut half a centimetre deep to take the cord, and a little thicker at the other, which is hollowed out for about one centi-metre to take the head of the weapon. Splitting of the wood at the ends is, as usual, prevented by binding the shaft with *gnetum* fibres, twisted into thread and waxed with beeswax.

The efficiency of the harpoon depends on the double-strand cord, extremely strong, made from *Hibiscus* fibres. One end is fixed on to the shaft, five centimetres from the point at which the fore-shaft enters it, and the other to the foreshaft, two centimetres from the base, with a thirty-two centimetre loop of cord between the two fixings.

The harpoon blade, now made of iron, is eleven centimetres long and spear-shaped, ending in a series of barbs. The haft of the blade is bound tightly on to the short foreshaft, also eleven centimetres long, which is scraped thin at the end so that the haft can be bound on smoothly. The complete weapon mounted for use is about eighty-eight centimetres long overall in the Onges and Jarawas, and slightly shorter, about sixty-five centimetres, in the Arioto.

To prepare the harpoon for use the slack of the cord is wound firmly round the shaft, and the foreshaft with the blade attached is forced in. As the harpoon strikes, the shaft becomes detached and the victim, firmly held by the barbed arrow head, drags it along on the end of the cord until it catches in the undergrowth and holds the animal fast.

There is little difference between the arrow harpoons of Little Andaman and Great Andaman, and what difference there is affects only the dimensions, the type of cord, and the form of the barbs. The basic principle remains the same wherever it is found; all the Negritos, including the Semang and Aetà still use it, although these

two have added feathers, and poisoned tips, in imitation of neighbouring peoples.

For the capture of large fish and animals such as turtles, dolphins
and dugong, the Onges and Arioto use not the arrow harpoon but
the spear harpoon. Brown saw none of these among the Onges he
studied in Rutland, and consequently assumed its absence on Little
Andaman. The Onges carry as little as possible on their sea voyages
for the sake of speed, and would not therefore take spear harpoons
(used only for marine hunting) with them on trips to Rutland,
which they visit only for the purpose of hunting pigs and not to
fish, or to hunt marine animals. They certainly have, and use, spear
harpoons even today; I myself have been with the Onges and seen
their harpoons used from the canoes. I had ample opportunity to
admire both the effectiveness of the weapons and the accuracy of
the throwers.

The greater structural and operational simplicity of the spear
harpoon, in comparison with the arrow harpoon, leads one to
suppose it the older of the two. Its cord is made of tough *Hibiscus*
fibres, and with the aid of these and a straight shaft about six metres
long and little over four centimetres in diameter, even the humblest
of nails, seven centimetres long and three millimetres in diameter,
can become the point of a spear harpoon. It is fixed into the shaft
(usually of mangrove wood) which is hollowed out at the thinner
end to take it, and with a cord up to a hundred metres long or more
attached to the nail two centimetres from the head, the spear harpoon is ready for use – shaft, point and cord.

When the harpoon is to be used for turtles, no barbs are needed,
as the point is driven so firmly into the shell that blocks of wood
have to be carried in the canoes to knock it out for re-use.

The harpoon throwers stand ready on the platform jutting out
fore and aft of the canoes (see p. 122), the free end of the cord is tied
to one of the booms to prevent it being jerked out of the canoe as
the victim tries to escape, and the slack is coiled in the bottom of
the canoe. The thrower holds the cord against the harpoon as he
waits for the right moment and then throws. As the harpoon strikes,
the point detaches from the shaft, which floats on the water till
picked up – often to be used as a punt-pole in the shallow waters of
the coral reefs as the canoe follows the victim, now held firmly on
the end of the cord.

The widespread use of the arrow and spear harpoons since very ancient times is evidenced by their survival in areas far removed from each other, and among primitive peoples geographically completely isolated. The arrival of the harpoon in the Andamans must in all probability have occurred thousands of years ago when it was widespread at least in the south and south-east of the Asian continent. Even the Andamanese canoes with their platforms fore and aft built specially for the harpoon throwers indicate not only the antiquity of the islanders, but also their historical and cultural connection with the peoples represented today by the few remaining Negritos.

From the evidence of the middens it is clear that the links between the Onges and the Jarawas are very close. While the date of the first migration from Little Andaman to Great Andaman remains uncertain there can be no doubt that migrations took place, followed by isolation within the islands, until today the Arioto cannot understand the Eremtaga, and the Onges neither the Jarawas nor the Sentinellese. There is very little in the literature on the Jarawas and their origin, but from my own observations I would deduce that they arrived in Great Andaman comparatively recently, as even their subsequent rigid isolation has not brought about any really essential cultural differences from the Onges.

The route of the migration will undoubtedly have led them via Rutland, whose heights can be seen as an open invitation from the north of Little Andaman. Chains of small, uninhabited islands lie between; the Onges have a name for all of them and have camp sites there for use on hunting or fishing expeditions; the Arioto, on the other hand, do not appear ever to have been to the islands. From Rutland migrations would have moved on to Great Andaman, until, filtering through to the extreme north, they became the Jarawas, or 'strangers', as the Arioto still call them. The Arioto themselves probably arrived previously by the same route but stopped in the coastal areas, then uninhabited and inviting occupation. The Arioto would have considered themselves owners of the still uninhabited areas and tried to exclude later immigrants; so began the hostility I have already described between the occupiers of the coasts and the later arrivals whom they forced into the depths of the forests.

All the evidence points to this being far more than mere supposition and even today the Onges persist in their tendency to expand towards the north. In 1953 I could find no trace of a number of Onges whom I had known in 1952; the others told me they were all 'dead', but it seems probable that they had migrated to the islands further north. And in 1954 nearly all the canoes belonging to the communal huts in the south-west of Little Andaman, which I had seen in 1953, had vanished and were said to have gone with the 'dead'. It is probable that they too had migrated to Great Andaman, becoming 'Jarawas'.

This is physically quite possible. Between Little Andaman and Great Andaman the Onges have a line of transit camps, still in use, where food and water are easily available. All have a name, and I followed the line myself. With the help of their fragile but very fast canoes, and without carrying food or water (which they know will be available at the next transit camp), they can travel very quickly. They take fire with them in the canoes in the form of a burning torch and while they are at sea, unlike the lazy pace of their normal attitude to life, they seem possessed by the desire to reach the next stopping point on terra firma.

Moreover, one may deduce from the fact that the names of these transit camps are all in the Onge language that the migrations have always been from south to north. Little Andaman, formed as it is mainly of coral banks and only projecting a short way above the sea, disappears from view in the tropical mists a few kilometres from the shore; from Rutland it is invisible, and as the Andamanese only travel by sea with land in sight or when its existence and direction is well known, no one from the north would have dared to travel south into the unknown.

We have already seen that the ignorance of the present-day Jarawas as regards the sea is no bar to a hypothesis of their original arrival in Great Andaman by sea. Colebrook, a hundred and fifty years ago, actually saw them with canoes, and Gilbert Rogers[1] recorded seeing canoes on the coasts of North Sentinel very similar to those of the Onges today. The accumulation, therefore, of this evidence and the general similarity of culture throughout the archipelago all adds up to inescapable conclusions.

Even the unique dances enjoyed by the Onges are to be seen

[1] *Andaman and Nicobar Gazetteer*, 2 January 1904.

among the Jarawas, with the characteristic marking of the rhythm by slapping the calves against the buttocks. This does not seem to have been a feature of the Arioto dances, in which the rhythm was by the *pukuta yemnga*, a kind of convex shield made of the very hard and aromatic red wood (*Pterocarpus dalbergoides*) which the termites never seem to attack. I was able to obtain one of these shields, the last that the twenty-three surviving Arioto possessed and the only musical instrument in the islands. It is played by one man with his feet, while the dancers, male and female, form lines on each side of him a short distance away. Before use the convex face is decorated with lines of white ochre and chains of tusk shells are hung from a hole at the end opposite to the one on which the player's feet beat; from the same hole runs a cord, which he holds in his hand to prevent the instrument moving away from him as he beats. The players change from time to time as the dancers shuffle on and on for hours in the light of the resin torches. But apart from the instrument itself, the rhythmic hand-clapping and the dancers singing in unison are the same throughout the Andamans.

The women clap their hands in rhythm, and then slap one thigh with the open palm of one hand, the other hand clasping the wrist, singing all the time. The men dance in Indian file, beating the ground first with the right heel, then with the left, the toes barely raised from the ground, moving a short way forward each time. As they dance they lean forward, then with hands clasped and their fingers interlaced. There are variations, but the basic step is always the same.

One difference between the Onges and the Jarawas is that in the latter both sexes are naked, while the Onge women have in recent times adopted the *naquineghe* or apron. Complete nudity was a characteristic of all the Negritos, including the Semang and Aetà, and the Jarawa migrations probably took place before the introduction of the *naquineghe*.

The present inability of the three peoples to understand each other is more a question of pronunciation than of difference in actual words. To examine the question fully it would be necessary to collect a large number of words and analyse their affinity; meanwhile we know that despite their inability to understand each other there is a close resemblance between the language of the Jarawas and Sentinellese and that of the Onges. Strict isolation can lead to comparatively rapid variation and it is now difficult to establish their linguistic connections outside the Andamans, but Africa can certainly be discounted, in view of the general weight of evidence against any Negro ancestry.

Like the Onges the Jarawas are divided into endogamous groups, each with its own name, corresponding to their communal huts, and each with their own territory for the purposes of hunting, fishing and gathering food. There is little reliable information about their daily life or even their numbers; it is, however, certain and I cannot overstress this, that the Jarawas are Negrito in type,[1] with the same admixture as in the Onges.

Whoever or whatever they may be, the replacement of primitive expeditions by genuine attempts at pacification would, quite apart from the obvious humanitarian considerations involved, afford a unique opportunity for detailed study of a dying population in regeneration, and the refusal of an otherwise irrevocable progress towards final extinction.

But the problem of the Jarawas is merely one aspect of the problem of the Andamanese in general, and their connection with the Negritos both past and present. The Semang and the Aetà, as we have seen, resemble each other, and together resemble the Andamanese, in a number of essential points. Recent contacts with other influences in Malacca and the Philippines respectively have produced variations – such as the Semang use of traps and snares with which they take small animals, and also birds, which the Andamanese never touch. They have also taken to making refuges in the trees as a defence against wild animals, non-existent in the Andamans. Traps, poison, agriculture, fish-hooks, animal nets, are all late acquisitions, not found among the original Negritos. It was thought by Brown that spears, used by the Semang, were also unknown among the peoples of the Andamans, but I have myself seen them used by the Onges, though admittedly I saw only a few, and very rough specimens; I did, however, manage to bring some back with me.

In the case of the canoes, the Semang and the Aetà seem to have

[1] On 11 January 1951 a Jarawa was killed at Lekeralarta on Middle Andaman and the head is now in the Indian Museum in Calcutta. This head shows signs of beard, unlike those of two Jarawas held in the Nicobars since the September 1938 incident. Short, muscularly well-developed, strong and very black, Jarawas are normally beardless, as is usual in Negritos.

completely lost the art of building them, probably by the same mechanism as the Jarawas, that is as a result of isolation in forest areas. The Semang sometimes prepare hasty bamboo rafts when they want to cross a river, however, and there do appear to be a few canoes among groups of Aetà living along the coasts. Facility of contact with neighbouring areas has brought about modification in both peoples, especially in the course of the last hundred years, whereas the complete isolation of the Andamans cannot be over-stressed.

These later contacts, however, have not yet destroyed the ancient physical and cultural habits of the Semang and Aetà. The food of those who have remained nomadic in the forest still consists of roots, fruit, and whatever they can get by hunting and fish-ing. Some have certainly recently tended to settle, and have adopted a rude form of agriculture, but the rest have remained as primitive as the peoples of the Andamans, using digging sticks to get at the edible roots, and hooked sticks to get at the fruits on the trees. They do have axes with blades (now made of iron) which can split open tree-trunks to get at the honey inside or, when hafted on the end of a stick, to hollow out trunks to make vessels and clean off the exterior. But again, their bows and arrows, very similar to the ancient pattern, still remain their chief means of acquiring food.

The Negritos of Malacca and the Philippines make baskets, some of which are clearly copied from neighbouring peoples, while others correspond to the basketwork of the Andamans. The Onges, the finest of the Andaman basket workers, have two types of basket, one intended to last and one made purely for some tem-porary purpose. When they are on hunting or gathering trips out-side Little Andaman they will hastily construct roughly made carriers for whatever they find. Anyone who saw, for example, these rough baskets on Rutland would assume reasonably enough that the Onge baskets are inferior to those of the peoples of Great Andaman, but in fact these purely temporary carriers, intended to be thrown away after their immediate use, are extremely well made. They are plaited over a frame of solid reeds, about two and a half centimetres in diameter, and split in half longways. The split reeds are arranged and tied in a star position to give the base and then bent upwards, the ends being joined to a circle of split reed, which forms the rim of the basket. Long ribbons of bark stripped from anything handy are then woven over the frame, the size of the mesh being determined by the nature of the contents for which it is intended; the basket merely has to get the haul back to the camp, and is then thrown away. The real Onge baskets, however, are made with great care and are never carried on these expeditions. They resemble the traditional Semang and Aetà baskets, now abandoned in favour of foreign types.

CHAPTER FIVE

Harvest of Honey

The climate of the Andamans favours other things besides luxuriant vegetation. Myriads of insects and other tiny creatures are everywhere. The most important, and most dangerous for Europeans, are the mosquitoes, although the Andamanese are not worried by them. The most common is *Anopheles ludlowi*. These never move voluntarily more than a kilometre from their breeding ground, but the winds often carry them further afield.

On Little Andaman I saw five different species of flies. Their larvae fed just as well on vegetable refuse as on meat. I remember throwing away on the shore north of Labanar a coconut from which I had drunk the milk; two days later I found the inner pulp, still soft, crawling with larvae, which later turned into flies very like our own. By contrast on another occasion I noticed that a beautiful green and yellow lobster weighing two kilograms which was thrown up on to the beach did not sustain larvae.

In various places round the shores of the Andamans the so-called sand-flies are a considerable nuisance, even in the day time and in full sun. Although only two millimetres long, the bite of these blood-thirsty insects causes unbearable irritation for some days. Even dousing oneself in Flit has no effect. If one goes into the darkness of the foliage to escape them, where it is damp, one is at once attacked by leeches. Only complete destruction of the vegetation would eradicate them and the ticks and this is unthinkable. The Onges with their bare plastered bodies are reasonably well protected, however, and the fleas also seem put off.

On Little Andaman I encountered too the ravages of bright yellow ants, diaphanous and so small one could hardly see them, which invaded our stores of provisions and my collections, despite every precaution. Holes so small that a hair would hardly pass through presented no obstacle to them and the metal boxes with tightly fitting lids, in which I kept my insect specimens, proved mouse- and rat-proof but not ant-proof, with disastrous results. Everything they found edible was reduced to dust. Sugar attracted them most of all; it was no use keeping it in screw-top containers, apparently foolproof, as they merely crawled up the thread of the lid and reduced the sugar to a mass of bodies. Large sheets of drawing paper left on top of a box for a fortnight were soon perforated by innumerable holes, through which they laid eggs, covering the sheets underneath. When I turned the top sheet over I found the eggs underneath, tended by myriads of adult ants, so small that a few puffs were enough to blow them off. On the ground all one could see were tiny dots – the eggs – apparently motionless; but almost immediately these all disappeared, borne away by the invisible workers. Not one egg was left behind. No other animal would have been able, if disturbed, to recover every one of its eggs like these ants and carry them off to safety; some sort of corporate organization among them seems to be proof against any threat of danger.

Another species which I saw around Labanar were the so-called red ants of the tropics, *Oecophylla smaragdina*. They were everywhere and I was able to observe them closely both in the day time and at night. I first made the acquaintance of these terrible but wonderful creatures on my first landing on Little Andaman on 20 February 1951, with Dr S. S. Sarkar. In the absence of any Onges, and not knowing anything of the enemies waiting among the leaves, we approached the foliage near the shore. In a flash vicious red ants whose nest we had kicked under the leaves forced us to the defensive. We escaped unharmed, but I was fascinated by them.

True to their popular name, they are red, but a very pale colour, verging on gold, although the species also includes some black specimens (the males) and some of a brilliant green (the queens). To see these one has to break the nest open; only the red warlike workers are normally visible. Their bodies, little more than one centimetre long, are borne on long, graceful legs, which are always in frenzied motion day and night. One only has to approach an isolated ant going about its work on the ground or on the leaves (or even worse, about the nest) and it will fly into absolute paroxysms of rage. I was much amused by the pugnacity of those apparently insignificant creatures. The ones nearest to the intruder always stretch forward as far as they can towards him on their middle and back legs, heads raised, their two front legs threshing the air feverishly, as though desperate to get at the invader at the earliest possible moment. They strain every nerve to reach forward and as they do so even lower parts of the abdomen reach over towards the enemy ready to sting. No matter how big he is they will attack, and their pygmy rage becomes quite comical. Once they have found bare flesh they bite madly, bringing their sting down viciously at the same time.

They can even distinguish between clothes and bare skin and will run about like lightning in search of a place to sting. They can cover a man completely from head to foot in a few seconds. The two phases of the attack, the straining of the body towards the enemy and the actual biting and stinging, are repeated frenziedly over and over again, the smell of blood seeming to whip them up to further rage. Nevertheless, I could not help thinking how graceful and elegant these fascinating creatures were and it would be well worth while returning to Little Andaman to film their life cycle and bellicose habits.

Oecophylla smaragdina belongs to a group of 'weaver' ants found particularly in the tropics of Asia and Oceania. These sew leaves together to build their nests; as they work only at night it is difficult to observe them, but they can be made to weave in the day time simply by making a hole in the nest. Repair begins immediately. They use a substance formed in the salivary glands of the larvae, which emerges like silk thread and hardens in contact with the air. In the day time, with the heat of the sun and the drier atmosphere hardening occurs too quickly, which is why they prefer to work at night: an outstanding example of adaptation to the necessities of the situation.

After a series of observations, I managed to reconstruct the process by which they work. When they went to join two leaves, they form gangs of seven or eight workers to draw selected leaves from a healthy plant together. The workers form a chain, one behind the other, each holding the one in front of him in his mandibles, with the rear ant clinging to one leaf and the front ant ready to grasp the edge of another leaf and draw it to him. A series of these chains, working side by side with their efforts synchronized, are strong enough to draw two leaves together, all the heads of the chains gripping one leaf in their jaws and the rear pairs of feet clinging with their tiny, sharp hooks on to the other. If the two leaves are growing close together, a single row of ants side by side is enough and they seem instinctively to know how many are needed.

Once the edges are together, the weaving squad can begin work. Each ant is armed with a larva gripped tightly in its jaws, moving it to and fro like a shuttle so that the fine thread of liquid emerges over the joint between leaves, hardening almost before it reaches them. And so the 'weaving' with the larvae 'shuttles' continues until in the end the two leaves are joined firmly, one party holding the leaves together while the other joins them with the silken web. This is repeated until enough leaves are joined together in a sphere to form the nest, any odd gaps remaining being sealed with further layers of thread.

The weaving is done only by the hordes of workers, who are completely sterile throughout their life (the single queen enclosed with a few males in each colony lays the eggs). The amazing thing is that there appear to be no leaders superintending the work, or deciding what must be done at any given moment. Yet the work proceeds smoothly and silently, with no interruptions, as though done by a single craftsman, each ant obeying while none commands.

Equally fascinating, and far more destructive, are the termites, whose life cycle and activities are the same all over the world. The Onges' communal huts, which would otherwise last for a considerable time, are constantly ravaged by them and reduced to dust under their onslaught. Their annual swarms are much the same on Little Andaman as elsewhere. Clouds of them rise out of the ground when the rains come and in mid-April every year I used to see myriads of them attracted by the lights of my camp on the northeast coast of the island. They would swarm round the camp, many landing on the table in front of me, while thousands more piled up on the ground below. The moment they landed they stopped dead, firmly planted on all six legs as though paralysed, and arched the lower part of their body up and over their back, touching their four wings one after the other with the tip of the abdomen. The wings suddenly dropped off along a predetermined line of fracture, two to the left and two to the right. The whole process seemed to be some instinctive reflex movement triggered off by coming to land after the flight from their original hill. Then the termites began to walk quickly as though they had never had wings.

The casting of their wings is the signal for the males to look for the females. There follows a long nuptial 'march' culminating in the union of queen and males, identical with what I had seen among African termites, thousands of miles away.

Wherever they are, termites have a considerable effect on the vegetation; some plants flourish with the constant upheaval of the earth by the termites, while others cannot thrive in soil which is constantly turned over. Termite hills may consequently be quite bare of vegetation or covered with a dense jungle, according to species and location. It is most unwise to disturb a termite hill. A horde of defenders instantly assails the enemy, attacking him remorselessly with pincer-like jaws; if an attacking termite is pulled off its prey, the abdomen comes off in one's fingers leaving the head still attached to the victim, the jaws still biting viciously. Repair of the damaged hill begins immediately it is disturbed, tightly packed hordes of workers pouring out of the nest to the damaged area. Somehow news of the disaster spreads like wildfire throughout the hill, however large it may be, and like the red ants they obey implicitly some unexpressed order, following an instinct the mechanism of which is still quite unexplained.

The first impression of these hordes of repair workers is one of utter confusion, but in the mass of termites bumping into each other and apparently rushing about aimlessly each is motivated by one thing only – the repair of the nest as quickly as possible. Since termites need cover and darkness, this is done preferably with earth brought from inside the nest; but if necessary gangs of workers, chosen by some unknown mechanism from among the milling hordes, come out into the baking sun, contrary to all their instincts, and work from the outside, sacrificing themselves for the community.

Much remains to be learnt of this weird compelling mechanism, and I hope that others will be able to continue my observations in the Andamans, where there are endless opportunities for the uninterrupted study of these and other insects.

In sharp contrast to the termites, with their highly developed social structure, is the solitary life of the fly-eating Hymenoptera. I saw one for the first time in my camp near Labanar. My Indian porters had put up a clothes-line and as soon as the washing had been taken down, the lines immediately became covered with flies; suddenly, as though attracted by the easy prey one of these insects appeared as if by magic. Half flying, half jumping, fluttering its wings very characteristically the whole time, it went from one end of the line to the other in pursuit of flies. Many of them managed to escape, only to alight again on the line and be chased a second time. In an instant they were seized and swallowed.

Smaller, but equally numerous, are various kinds of wasps, and their presence enabled me to continue some observations I had begun in Italy. Wasps look after their larvae very carefully, continuously putting food into the mouths of the dumpy, wiggling creatures. The larvae are in fact so voracious, continually thrusting their heads out of their cells for food, that they will accept food offered to them on the point of a needle, especially if the 'nurses' are removed from the nest.

Wasp larvae secrete silk like those of the red ants, but it is used only to seal the aperture of the cell in which the larvae grow. The sealing occurs spontaneously, in the day time or at night, at precisely the right stage of larval development, and takes about half an hour. The silk is ejected from the mouth, very fine and shining in the sun, and hardens almost immediately into a tiny white dome, closing the aperture of the cell. The larva inside then passes into the chrysalis stage and emerges as an adult wasp. To get out of the cell the young wasp attacks the centre of the seal with its mandibles, not just tearing it away, but actually eating it, so that its own silk becomes its first adult meal. Once emerged, it is at once ready to take its place in the work of tending new generations of larvae. It begins by passing the food brought into the nest by the workers to the young larvae, receiving the food in its mouth from the foragers and passing it to the next generation. And so the eternal cycle continues.

Besides the wasps, two varieties of bee are found on Little Andaman, the larger, yellow *Apis dorsata* and the smaller brown *Apis nigrocinta*. The former, common in Central and Southern India and the Malaysian archipelago, builds large nests, hanging from the branches of trees. Its honey is the best, clear and golden, though less plentiful and containing a great deal of wax, and is greatly prized by the Onges. The darker bees, common in China, Celebes, Borneo and beyond, build their nests in cavities in the rocks, or in tree-trunks. Their honey, darker and with less wax, is more plentiful, but not so fine; when there is enough of the golden honey the Onges ignore the darker variety.

Few of the fruits on Little Andaman contain much sugar, but the Onges eat more than enough honey to compensate any deficiency that would otherwise occur. Whatever the fruit in season, men, women and children climb happily about like acrobats, hanging in the trees to get at it and the honey that goes with it. To chop the tree down is, of course, easiest and the obvious first choice for any Onge. Failing this, and their hooked poles, they climb up the nearby lianas into the branches, or walk up the trunk – an easy feat for them with their very long arms and almost prehensile toes.

Although there are arak nuts and betel leaves in the forest, the Onges ignore them. They are the same variety as elsewhere; *Areca catechu* and *Piper betel*. The Nicobarese are so addicted to them that many have lips and teeth hideously deformed as a result, but this is quite unknown among the Onges, contrary to earlier reports. The appearance of addiction in the Nicobars may have occurred after the separation of the peoples.

With all these fruits the Onges consume vast quantities of honey from the two species of bee, *dorsata* and *nigrocinta*. During the rainy season they can only get at the darker, poorer honey of *nigrocinta*, which builds nests under boulders or in crevices of trees or rocks. The Onges' real honey orgies occur, therefore, in the dry season, when the honey birds (Indicationidae), common in Africa and all over Asia, lead them to the trees where the golden honey of *dorsata* is hidden.

When one of the Onges finds a nest of bees he puts a mark on the rock or tree as a sign of ownership. None of the others would then dare to take possession of it, for fear of punishment by the group,[1] but when the time comes to take the honey everyone helps in the hard work of getting at the nest and opening it up. On one trip from Labanar to Togalanghe, on 19 March 1954, the Onges pointed out over twenty *Nigrocinta* nests to me, all reserved ready for use

[1] However deep in the forest a crime is committed, it will inevitably be discovered in the end, and punished by banishment from the community.

when the supply of *dorsata* diminished at the onset of the stormy season, when the gales lashing the branches dislodge the nests and hurl them to the ground.

Unlike the beekeepers of the civilized world, the Onges make no attempt to protect their bare bodies while they are extracting honey. Yet they are never stung, and watching them one felt in the presence of some age-old mystery, lost by the civilized world. I watched an Onge from the ground with my field glasses as he climbed up a tree to a *dorsata* nest and saw him, as it were, blowing on the bees round about the trunk as he went up. As he approached the nest they huddled round it in a protective cloud, hiding it completely from view. Suddenly, as the Onge's face came within twenty centimetres of the boiling, humming mass, the bees seemed to shrink back as he blew on them. Not one moved to attack as he gouged out the combs with his bare hands, throwing handfuls of bees out into the air. And then the whole cloud of bees gathered into a swarm and left the tree and the nest to the interloper.

The Onge stripped lengths of green bark from the lianas growing up the tree, and then broke the nest up. Tying the combs to his back with the strips of bark he lowered himself down to the ground, swinging like an ape from liana to liana. There, while his friends fell on the honey, he calmly cleaned himself down – with not one sting on him. This he did in a way unusual for the Onges, filling his mouth with water from a nearby pond and squirting it into his cupped hands, until he had enough in his hands for a perfunctory rub down. This method of washing is common in primitive peoples but advanced for the Onges. When they have been painting themselves with the usual fat and ochre paste, for example, the women will clean their hands to their satisfaction by wiping them on their *naquineghe*, while the men use the dogs' coats as a convenient towel.

In March 1952, in the middle of the honey season, I was on the west coast of Little Andaman, near Nachuge. Twelve Onges were with me, and when they noticed a bees' nest high up in a *Pterocarpus* the youngest of them at once climbed up after it. As soon as he saw that the combs were full of honey, with no larvae, he called for a container. With amazing speed he tore enough bark off the nearest liana with his teeth to make a cord over twenty metres long and the hollowed-out log was soon hauled up, to come down again crammed with combs brimming with pale golden honey, very sweet, and delicately flower-scented. No one waited for the climber to reach the ground. With my men and the Onges the party numbered twenty-two in all, every one of them hungry. The log was thirty centimetres across, and besides the combs there was a good four inches of honey in the bottom, but even so I only managed to set aside two litres for the man who did all the work, before the combs had all disappeared and the remaining liquid as well. The whole lot was gone in a matter of minutes.

What puzzled me was how the bees were quietened. I knew from personal observation that both the varieties of bee on Little Andaman could and did sting badly, and I knew that the Onges I had watched had done nothing deliberately to avoid stings.

In Man, the olfactory sense can detect minute amounts of iodoform, for example, but we are completely insensitive to other substances strongly repellent to flies, mosquitoes and other insects. Some similar mechanism must also operate in the case of bees. The Onges cannot understand anything of this, but they must possess some age-old, almost intuitive and innate knowledge, which they apply unconsciously. At some time someone must have found that the juice of a certain plant they call *tonjoghe*, apparently inodorous, has the power of deterring bees, and this knowledge, handed down from generation to generation, is applied with delightful simplicity.

In the forests of Little Andaman there are bushes of *tonjoghe* everywhere, and the Onge who is to go after the honey simply grabs a handful of the leaves and stuffs them into his mouth. With some vigorous chewing they are quickly reduced to a greenish pulp, which is smeared all over the body, particularly the hair. Another huge mouthful chewed on the way up and spat at the bees to make quite sure that they will be deterred even to the point of failing to attack the unsmeared bystanders. I have myself tried the leaves, and like the Onges found them quite tasteless and odourless. The Onges say that the 'magic' was revealed by a seer, and it is a curious fact that of all the luxuriant vegetation on the island only this one plant is effective.

I am unfortunately not in a position to say definitely to what species *tonjoghe* belongs. I took some plants to Port Blair, where they were planted in the Governor's garden; unfortunately before they could flower the then Governor left, and a new gardener thought they were weeds and pulled them up. I never managed to see the plant in flower in the wild state, as this occurs at the height of the rainy season, and as no final definition is possible in the absence of the flower it remains unidentified.

The Onges take full advantage of the plant's properties as a bee-deterrent and in mid-March they eat honey, paint themselves, and dance, twenty-four hours a day. During these orgies I have seen a group of about sixty Onges demolish in a few days ten pigs and a dozen large, wooden vessels full of honey, with basket after basket of fish, caught every night by the women, who were apparently not in the least tired by the long daily treks into the forest after the honey. I can never look back on the Onges without a feeling of profound respect for their powers of digestion!

Yet another source of food for the islanders is the cicada. On Little Andaman there are a few species a little larger than the European variety and others rather smaller. The Onges collect the pupae as they emerge from the ground, usually in the mornings, and roast them as a great treat. They are actually very clean insects, which develop slowly under the earth over a period of years sucking lymph from the roots of the trees. When they emerge from the ground the pupae become leathery, but this presents no problem to the indomitable teeth of the Onges. Inside the cicada chrysalids are a mass of delicate tissues, so white and clean that one can understand the Onges' predilection for them.

On Little Andaman the cicadas chirp intermittently, with long silences; most of the day one hears nothing of them and when they suddenly start up the Onges fall absolutely quiet, terrified of frightening them away and losing their chrysalids.[1] In a few moments the whole forest suddenly echoes with a chorus of cicadas, as they all start up as one and then, a minute later, fall silent. Their intermittent chirping is not confined to the Andamans; it is a feature of several species throughout southern Asia. At Golpahar when I was in the middle of the forest excavating kitchen-middens I heard cicadas start up every day at 6.30 p.m., and then stop until the following day. In the mountains of South India, on the slopes

---

[1] The Onges do not seem to share the superstitions reported by Man and Brown among the Arioto, who appear to believe in fantastic connections between cicadas, the sun, and storms.

of Pushpaghiri ('mountain of the flowers'), I saw workmen using the cicadas to mark the end of their shift, so regular were they in starting up. The whole valley echoed with their chirping for three minutes, and promptly at the signal everyone stopped work.

As well as cicada chrysalids, the Onges love the white larvae of the long-horned grasshoppers (Tettigonidae) which are common all over the island. They are the size of a man's finger and the larvae, like those of the cicadas, feed exclusively on vegetable matter and are very tasty. I have watched the Onges collecting them and managed to see something of the life cycle of the Long-horns. Both the larvae and the chrysalids live in cylindrical holes in trees, which the larvae bore out by eating at the wood. Before turning into a chrysalis the larva prepares the way out for the adult insect, which is less well adapted for gnawing. The chrysalids them-selves seem determined to take up as little space as possible; as in all the Longhorns the future elytra are clearly visible on the crea-ture's back, with the membranous wings, and the three pairs of legs are always curled up, with the first and second pairs very close to each other. The third pair is further away, clearly so as to balance the embryonic antennae. These are very long and spring from the sides of the head, passing down on either side of the thorax, be-tween the first and second pairs of legs, to finish neatly coiled in front of the thorax, touching the elytra and the second pair of legs. Curled up like this into two or three coils, according to sex, the thread-like, whitish antennae look like intestinal worms inside the chrysalids. Each pair of legs lies motionless against the thorax, the feet touching in a precise line down the centre of the body. When the creature wakes from its long sleep, all the parts unfold, and the elytra and other external parts harden and colour according to the species. A new stage in the life cycle, shorter but more intense, has begun.

The Onges are not interested in the mole-crickets, but I found them fascinating. It is known that animals can find their nests or their usual haunts even if they are moved quite considerable dis-tances away and deliberately confused, but the mechanism is not yet fully understood. It is likely that the same mechanism operates whether in the air, or on the ground, or below ground. The mole-cricket, for example digs long galleries underground and does not often come out into the open. The galleries are interconnected, enabling fair distances to be covered underground. It is not difficult to catch a mole-cricket, mark it, put it on the ground some distance away, and then recapture it in the original place. As it travels underground, sight can play no part in the mechanism, and in fact it burrows down as soon as it is put down on the ground. Its tunnels are not far down, and are easily damaged by heavy rain, animals or human feet, and so on. When this happens the insect closes the entrance to the damaged tunnel and digs a new one parallel to it, digging connecting galleries to the other tunnels, and it will do this, however many times the tunnel is damaged, as though determined to keep to the same line of direction.

Very different are the fireflies, which gave me a strange experience at the beginning of March 1953. I was with some Indians on a hunting expedition at low tide among the mangrove swamps near Berié-Abdalù on the east coast of Little Andaman. Night fell while we were still in the swamps, suddenly, as it always does in the tropics. There was a mist, and encouraged by the exceptional stillness of the air a shower of lights suddenly appeared all round us, twinkling in the air and on every leaf, as far as the eye could see, lit as if by magic. The effect was even more vivid than the phosphorescence of the sea that I had often admired. A confusion of strange sparks of light passed silently to and fro, and some of the city-bred Bengalis were terrified. To quieten them, I called them to a nearby plant, which was glowing like all the rest. As we approached we could see thousands of tiny specks of light moving endlessly to the edges of the leaves and branches and darting off into the air. I had seen fireflies before in a number of places but even so I could not take my eyes off these clouds of them, massed on every leaf and twig in sight.

The Onges, with their fear of the darkness, never see the fireflies in the mangrove swamps; but at certain times of the year there are millions of them round their camps and curiously enough the islanders attach no special significance to them. Every spring I spent in the island I saw fireflies, but not in large numbers. These were the males, which are winged, unlike the females. Once they reach the forest, they soar so high into the air that it is impossible to follow them, but the lights of the camp drew them down within sight. I never saw any females, easily distinguishable from the males as their light is continuous, whereas that of the males is intermittent. The constant flights of the males into the treetops made me think that the females were up there, but I was unable to confirm this. The fireflies will always remain for me one of the most attractive things about the forests of the Andamans.

One could write whole books about all the insects and their nightly concerts. On the *Ficus* of Little Andaman live the caterpillars of a very beautiful moth *Antherea paphia*, one of the Saturnidae; these are the silkworms which produce Tasar (or tussore) silk. On these trees they spin their silky cocoons, stronger than those of our European silkworms. Unlike the European *Saturnia pyri*, which leaves the plant before it goes into its cocoon, the Andaman variety remains on it. To avoid falling to the ground, the caterpillars always chew the leaves without weakening the edge to which they are clinging; one false nibble and they would plunge to the ground. As they enter the cocoon stage they take even greater precautions, crawling back to where the leaves join the stem and spinning a ring of silk in the joint. Then they run a thread down the dorsal vein of a leaf and attach the cocoon to it, so that even if the leaf is blown off by the gales the cocoon remains attached to the twig by its thread.

As the *Ficus* sheds its leaves in stages, and is therefore never entirely without leaves, the caterpillars appear twice a year, once in spring and once in the autumn. The butterflies from the first brood appear in mid-September and those from the second in mid-February, the only difference between the two broods, being the duration of the cocoon stage.

When it emerges from its cocoon the butterfly takes a few steps to the nearest support, where it spreads its wings to dry off. Then it sleeps for two days, waking in the night of the second day. As it sleeps the antennae, wire-like in the female, thicker in the male, lie flat against the head behind the eyes, becoming erect only as the butterfly wakes. The females are quiet and show no sign of flight, although they have large wings. The males, however, are restless, and keep circling, mating on their first flight. The females are usually fertilized and die as soon as they have laid their eggs on the plant where they were born. Virgin females which I kept in a case attracted males from many kilometres away, as with our *Saturnia pyri*. The males know unhesitatingly which are the virgin females, although it is not known how they do so.

For the greater part of the year crickets and frogs fill the nights with wave after wave of placid, homely sound, tenor and baritone in full and solemn chorus. Within one area of a few kilometres there are more crickets than the entire human population of the world. Only the males chirp; the females are silent. The song may be for the purpose of attracting the females, but I rather doubt this, for they sing not only before, but also during and after mating. Alone or in chorus crickets will always sing, right up to the moment of death.

The general rule in all the various species of cricket which I have collected in various parts of the world is that only the males chirp. Very rarely both males and females sing; in other rare cases, neither sex sings. However great the physical variations between the species, their mating habits vary very little.

In the Andamans, however, the noise even of the crickets is drowned by the amphibia, particularly the green frogs. Like the crickets, they never sing alone, but always in chorus, led by those with the loudest voice. At fairly regular intervals a few odd frogs will start up; sometimes the chorus is lost, but only for a short while, and then it returns in full force, drowning the individual singers. Is this their collective homage to the fair sex, the females choosing the champions who lead the choir? I do not myself consider this a satisfactory explanation; in the Andamans at least the females normally behave as though the singing does not exist, even while the males work themselves up into a frenzy of croaking.

I managed to collect fairly large numbers of all these vocal creatures, particularly the insects, for the Institute of Zoology of the University of Naples, and it appears that all are known species common in the neighbouring islands and land masses. Insects are easily spread by the wind over considerable areas if they are caught up in an air current while in flight; I remember one October in the Gulf of Guinea, over three hundred miles from the nearest land, I caught considerable numbers of large insects, blown towards the ship by the wind and attracted by the lights. Borne by the monsoon winds, the insects of southern Asia and Indonesia must have drifted across to the Andamans long ago and flourished in the lush forests.

Needless to say, the abundance of insect life on the Andamans makes the archipelago a birds' paradise. Like the insects on which they live their song echoes through the forests day and night, to the background rhythm of the woodpeckers tapping on the trunks. I knew that they did this when seeking food, but it was the Onges, natural observers of wild life, who convinced me that the tapping could sometimes be unconnected with foraging. Wherever I camped there were always large trees nearby and with the aid of field glasses it was a simple matter to keep an eye on the wood-peckers, which varied in size from some smaller than our sparrows to others, brilliantly coloured and bigger than pigeons.

One persistent tapper on Little Andaman is a beautiful black woodpecker with a bright red tuft on its head, *Dryocopus martius*, also found in Asia and parts of Europe. I captured some that were thirty-five centimetres long, bigger than any of the other local species. Another, equally common, was slightly smaller than our blackbird and a glorious chestnut colour all over. A little black and white one was even more numerous. I often saw a variety of *Dendrocopus major*, with black and white body, red tuft on the head and a striking crimson feather under the tail. Others were mainly green, always with the red tuft on the head.

All of them hammer on the tree-trunks with their beaks and it is not fully understood why they do so. Tapping in search of insects can be heard the year round and the sound is similar to that made when the nest is being hollowed out. The other form of tapping, true drumming in the musical sense of the word, is only heard in the mating season and is infinitely louder. The Onges connect this sound with reproduction, although they have not grasped the connection between mating and birth. It can be heard over three hundred metres away, while the tapping for food or nest-building carries only for a short distance.

When the bird is breaking through the bark in search of food or hollowing out the nest, the beak usually strikes the trunk at an angle and at irregular intervals. The bird throws its whole strength into each blow, lifting its head right back every time to strike even harder with the next blow. The blows are usually struck first from the right, three or four in quick succession, and then three or four from the left, to dislodge a chip of bark or wood. When the wood-pecker nears the larva he is after, still hidden under the bark, the blows may become perpendicular. In nest-building a hollow is cut out of wood, often seven or eight centimetres deep in the case of the larger species, and large enough in diameter to admit the bird. Then the hole is enlarged downwards, still the same width, for thirty centimetres or so, to end in an oval cavity large enough to take the incubating female. In both cases all the tapping is done while the bird clings on to the trunk with its claws, which have reversible digits; it is balanced by the tail with its hard, bristle-tipped feathers.

The musical drumming during the mating season is rhythmic, and less violent. The bird selects a hollow trunk and will return to the same one for months. The beak strikes at the rate of about seven to ten blows per second and always in one place, so that no bark is chipped out. The sound diminishes in intensity from the first blow to the last, unlike the food- or nest-drumming. Like the cicada the bird uses its own body as a sound box to aid reverberation, filling itself with as much air as possible. As part of the flight mechanism, all birds have air cavities connected to their lungs and in the woodpecker the system is extremely well developed. These cavities help to increase the vibrations made by drumming on the wood. The head is held at the right angle to obtain the best reverberation (not the best angle for chipping out bark, as when the bird is looking for food), and the bird itself vibrates with the wood, absorbing the short sound-waves and increasing the resonance.

Although to the naturalist there is enough in the wild life of the Andamans for endless studies of everything from cuckoos to parrots, sea snakes, shells with their beautiful spiral patterns – and the wealth of material almost overwhelms one – it must be admitted that the Onges see all the beauty around them mainly in terms of food.

They will search for hours for the nests of the salangana or *Collocalia esculenta*, the swallow which builds well-known edible nests so greatly prized in many parts of the world. The bird secretes a gummy saliva, which hardens when exposed to the air, and it is of this that it builds its nest in caves near the sea, ejecting saliva on to the roof of the caves. The substance acts in Man as an aphrodisiac, which may account for the value placed upon swallows' nests in China. The nests are found usually in the darkest parts of the caves, hanging from the roof, sometimes seven or eight in a bunch. It is not known why these swallows like to nest in the dark, or how they manage to find their own eggs and young when they return to the cave after foraging, or are driven away from the nest by intruders such as snakes. It seems on the face of it impossible for snakes to climb up the roof of the cave, but they do. I collected a number, all *Trimesurus viridis*, and now in the Institute of Zoology of the University of Genoa. I had to pull them off the roof by the tail, as they were stuck fast on the rough surface of the rock. The snakes devour both eggs and young of the swallows, but the parents invariably return to the right nest, even if the contents are gone. When disturbed the salangana, tiny insect-eating birds with very long wings, fly in a tight flock towards the mouth of the cave, where they can be easily knocked down or trapped.

Below the nests there is always a thick layer of guano, crawling with insects and built up over the centuries by generations of birds using the same nesting places. The nests, about five to six centimetres in diameter and very small inside, normally contain one egg, rarely two or three. When we detached the nests from the roof, the young, instead of trying to escape, clung fast to the nest with their claws, cowering in the bottom and staring at us.

To several nests with only one egg, I added another. When I returned a few days later I found the interloper being happily cared for by the foster parents, showing that as is usually the case the parent birds recognize only the nest and accept the contents of it without question. Outside the nest, however, they fail to recognize even their own offspring, and in carnivorous species may even eat them. The young of the salangana are tended by the parent birds for only a few days after hatching, and as soon as they begin to move about outside the nest all recognition is permanently lost.

It is somewhat surprising that the bird populations of the Andamans differ considerably from island to island. The establishment of such marked, almost specific differences as are now apparent between birds clearly originally of the same species must have taken a very long time indeed and can only be explained if one assumes – justifiably, from my observations – that many species roam less widely than one would expect. The pigeon of Little Andaman (*umughé* to the Onges) is surprisingly sedentary, so that varieties in the various islands have developed as isolates and differ considerably. That of South Andaman, for example, is smaller than that found on Little Andaman, while those of Car Nicobar are larger still. And in a particular area fifteen kilometres west of Port Blair I repeatedly caught pigeons which were absolutely emaciated with their intestines loaded with tapeworms, whereas outside this restricted area I never found one. Another pigeon, all white apart from the wings and tail, on the other hand, migrates regularly as far as Sumatra and Java, yet still fails to produce local species.

On the whole, there is considerable zoological and botanical uniformity between the two hundred and four islands in the archipelago, even the furthest apart. One striking feature is the complete absence of native large mammals and of any traces of such in the geological past. There are, for example, no felines except *Paradoxurus*, the jungle cat, rather smaller than the domestic cat, which lives along the coasts. It prefers marine prey and roams the beaches at night after fish and crustacea, leaving a long trail of footprints. Sometimes it will kill lobsters larger than itself, and in the morning one sees the remains that the sea has not washed away or the rats gnawed. This is significant, as the jungle cat and rats were clearly the only mammals on Little Andaman until the recent deliberate introductions, and it is interesting that the cat incidentally feeds and helps to perpetuate the rats on which it preys. Both, unlike the great mammals, have survived the gradual restrictions of area imposed by the continual fragmentation of the archipelago, by virtue of their greater adaptability to 'marine' existence. So, too, have the reptiles and amphibia managed to survive – all closely related to the species found on the land mass of which the Andamans were originally part.

In the case of amphibia many species have been cut off in the archipelago perhaps for thousands of years, and yet have nearly all remained identical with those of the continents from which they came. One example is *Bufo melanostictus*, the common toad of Asia. I found them the same on Great and Little Andaman as in Bengal, Assam, Ceylon and other parts of Asia, and unlike the birds there is no difference between the toad populations of the various islands.

The same is true of the reptiles except that the same species, in Asia highly poisonous, often lethal within an hour, are somewhat less poisonous in the Andamans, although they can still cause severe discomfort.

CHAPTER SIX

Food from the Sea

Around the islands, corals stretch out under the water, which is clear and transparent to a depth of several metres so that a riot of colour is clearly visible from the surface. Dazzling as the spectacle is, the first thing that strikes one is the sheer abundance of the coral: it grows slowly, and into the most fantastic shapes. The colours range from white to cream and brown, like leather, or to purple and brilliant blue in streaks tipped with vivid orange, always harmonious, as though gigantic multicoloured flowers have been scattered among the reefs.

Many of the corals are similar to those of the Mediterranean in colour and shape, but none have any commercial value for the traders, who look for highly ornamental effects. While the corals invade the rocks in endless masses wherever the water is clear, there are none at the mouths of the rivers. Here they are killed by the impurities brought down to the sea from inland after the floods. This explains the narrow, deep, channels running between the coral formations, corresponding to the flow from the river mouths. Along a coastline that stretches for well over a hundred kilometres I found only two of these channels, one in the north and one in the north-east of the island. Since their existence marks the absence of underwater coral reefs the Indian navy marked them with buoys in my presence in 1954.

All round Little Andaman the ebb tides reveal an expanse of coral reefs stretching as far as the eye can see, which are partially submerged for a few hours every day. Progress over these reefs is both difficult and dangerous. There are edges as sharp as glass everywhere, ready to pierce the skin at the slightest touch, and here and there submerged potholes, which vary in depth from three to six metres or more, with sudden vertical drops and dangerous overhangs. It is here, however, that underwater life is at its most beautiful. Swarms of fish, painted in fantastic variegated stripes, spots and patches in imitation of their surroundings, live among these caverns, rushing about in the wells of deep water. When they are pursued by bigger fish, the shoals will leap suddenly out of the water, only to be caught by the gulls who are always lying in wait for them. I have watched the shoals from the shore, and seen them leap out of the sea to lie gasping on the sand, dying quickly in the heat.

Where there are channels in direct communication with the open sea, small sharks slightly over a metre in length move in to meet any swimmers, though a clap of the hands is enough to put them to flight. Fish weighing several kilograms hide in the recesses of the rocks bordering the corals, but they quickly emerge if poked with a stick, and the Onge women have an ingenious system of catching them. Rocks sticking up out of the water swarm with crustacea and tiny molluscs. Apart from the crabs, I was struck by their poor relations, the hermit crabs, comical tenants of all kinds of shells. One species, common in Little Andaman but rare on Great Andaman, is a beautiful tomato red all over, while others are bluish or grey.

The underwater world round the islands is completed by large numbers of several Holothuria, lazy, but conspicuous, and the huge bivalve molusc, *Tridacna* or Giant Clam. Some of these are anything up to a hundred years old and well over a metre in diameter, and weigh between two and three hundredweight. Always open, and incapable of moving from place to place, they feed by means of a multicoloured 'fringe' attached to the hem of each shell, the beating cilia which wave unceasingly causing eddies in the surrounding water and so drawing in plankton from a wide radius. Under normally calm conditions, this process of drawing in and swallowing plankton goes on without stopping, day and night. The huge molluscs look like simple baskets of blue, red, green and white flowers set on the sea bed, but they are in fact terrible creatures. If a man's hand or a foot should be sucked into the quite strong eddy the 'fringe' of cilia immediately folds back and the *Tridacna* suddenly closes like a giant eye silently, viciously, and so violently as to crush completely the limb caught between the two valves as they close. The strength of *Tridacna* is terrifying; an Onge friend of mine lost all the toes of his right foot when he inadvertently touched a *Tridacna* while swimming under water, and they have even been known to cut a man in half. Unfortunately, the creatures do not require a great depth of water and are found a few metres from the surface, even in the highest tides, so that they are a real danger.

To describe the underwater life of the Andamans in detail would itself fill a book. The shells alone, monovalves and bivalves alike, are of innumerable kinds and would arouse the enthusiasm of any collector. Various kinds of elegant and brilliantly coloured cowries are everywhere, moving about slowly at the water's edge. In a few hours one can gather sackfuls of all kinds of perfect shells, each one more beautiful than the last.

Pterocera of various species abound among the reefs. They are always small, seldom reaching thirty centimetres including the strange finger-like protuberances which give them their name of 'finger-shells'. They are always drab and inconspicuous from above, but the inside of the shell is a beautiful coral red. But they are always easy to pick out because of their protuberances.

I myself learned a sharp lesson from a finger-shell. I had always wondered why the shell had so many of these apparently useless protuberances, and one taught me how wrong I was: these 'fingers' perform a vital function in the search for food. The finger-shell has a strong muscular foot, with which it closes its shell when it retreats inside. When the opening is closed, only the outer surface of the foot can be seen, like an operculum, brown and horny. The secret of the protuberances lies in their combined action with the propulsive power of the foot: this is capable of throwing the creature with great rapidity in any direction, but usually sideways. Once it has noticed an open bivalve, usually one of the many local pinnae, about thirty centimetres long, the *Pterocera* approaches cautiously and with a sudden rush thrusts one or two of its protuberances, usually the lateral ones, deeply into the aperture of the pinna. Once impaled, the bivalve, normally ready to barricade itself in its shell at the slightest touch, remains at the mercy of the *Pterocera*. The latter calmly prises open the blocked aperture, gradually inserting its prong deeper and deeper, and consumes the tender flesh of its helpless victim. (Another gastropod, *Murex fortispine*, uses a similar action on the larger bivalves. Its shell is equipped with a very effective form of tin-opener, which it keeps polished by vigorous rubbing.)

I watched a *Pterocera* attentively scrutinizing the hand holding it. After exploring it very carefully, the creature tried to free itself by beating violently with its foot, causing considerable pain. I held one by one of its protuberances, which was like a large right-angled hook. Suddenly, while my attention was held by a shoal of fish, I felt a sharp pain on the back of my hand. Taken by surprise, I watched the creature to try and discover what it had done. From a furrow at the base of one large front hook, a little to its left, I saw a tentacle emerge, able to turn in any direction, with a retractable eye at its tip. The eye, after a few exploratory movements, fixed its gaze on the place on my hand the creature intended to hit, and then the foot began to beat wildly on my hand, time and time again, causing a quite surprising degree of pain.

It is during the honey feasts, when the tides are exceptionally low and the seas calm, that the womenfolk come into prominence. While the men normally do all the hunting for game and large fish, using arrows and harpoons, the women, with their nets, catch the smaller fish in the rivers and marshes, and among the coral reefs at low tide. Their contribution to the everyday diet is by no means negligible, and during the season of very low tides their daily haul is tremendous.

The importance of fish to the Onges is shown by the fact that their word for it, *cioghe*, is also used to mean food in general, and clearly dates back to the time before the arrival of the pigs on the island, when fish and sea food in general was the basis of their diet. So plentiful is it that even at the height of the season the most they do in the way of preserving anything for future use is to expose the fish to smoke in order to deter flies from laying eggs on it for a day or two.

Only on very rare occasions do the men help in the net-fishing, and then only when they can completely fill the canoes with fish very quickly. I saw it happen for the first time on 24 March 1953, in the great coral reef near Nachuge, just as it happens all over the island at this time of year, when the pilchard shoals are so far inshore that there are not enough canoes to hold the catch. As the tide goes down, the shoals are caught in the reefs stretching out to sea all round the island and the Onges leave everything to man-handle the canoes from pool to pool and fill them to overflowing. The water is almost saturated with fish, and the Onges go on and on until they have nothing more they can use to hold the catch. No-where else in the world have I seen anything like this wholesale slaughter.

The pilchards of the Andamans are rather larger than usual, some weighing as much as half a kilogram or more. The Onges catch them regardless of size and then sort them into lengths before cooking (cooking, needless to say, without stopping to gut them). Men, women and children work feverishly, plunging their hands into the heaving mass of fish so that they reek of it for days, to-gether with the dogs, whose coats become the inevitable hand-towels.

Every available vessel is used for the cooking, and the rest of the haul is cooked directly over hot ashes. The biggest are cooked alone; the smaller ones, in batches of half to one kilogram, are wrapped in big fleshy leaves, tied up with vegetable fibres and cooked for ten minutes or so, turned regularly all the while. To boil the fish, an entire netful of fish roughly equal in size is plunged into boiling water, and boiled as usual far too long for our taste.

Everyone cooks and eats at the same time until (temporarily) unable to eat any more, when the rest of the haul is laid on im-provised racks with fires of green wood making smoke under-neath. When, a few days later, all is gone, fishing begins again. And so life goes on for weeks, until the shoals have passed the islands.

The real fishing, however, is done by the men. The women use small nets about fifty centimetres in diameter, and about the same depth. The opening consists of a pliable cane, barely three centi-metres in diameter, bent into a circle and tied with the ends crossing each other and projecting about twenty centimetres to form the handles. Each woman handles two nets, one held between the legs and the other in one hand, while the other hand pokes with a stick into the crevices in the reefs under the water to drive out the fish which have taken refuge as the tide goes out. Once found the fish are killed – very simply, by biting them between the eyes to crack their skulls – and thrown into the small basket every woman carries on her back, hung from the usual cord round her forehead.

The fish the women catch are all the varicoloured species which always haunt the coral shallows, bright red, blue, green, black and white in a wonderful range of stripes and patterns. The Onges eat them with no respect for design, and I must confess that I myself found them very good.

Besides fish, the women catch molluscs, crustacea, lobsters, crayfish, crabs and even some species of hermit crabs (the latter are baked alive in their adopted shells, and only the abdomen is edible). Lobsters are plentiful, some striped with green and blue and weighing up to half a kilogram, with a very delicate flavour, but the Onges do not seem to be greatly interested in them. They prefer fish and crabs; *Pterocera*, again baked alive, are great favourites and I quite saw why the kitchen-middens are full of *Pterocera* shells.

The men prefer to fish with bows and arrows made specially for the purpose, and very different from those intended for game, the shaft being made of very light hollow cane, instead of the solid wood demanded by the mechanics of the game-arrow. The fishing arrow is made of three parts, bound tightly into one. The point, now made of iron,[1] is about four to five millimetres in diameter and twenty to twenty-five centimetres long. Like that of the arrow harpoon, it is fixed by a tightly bound thread to a small stick or foreshaft about fifteen to twenty centimetres long and slightly smaller in diameter than the shaft proper (usually eighty to eighty-five centimetres long), so that the overall length of the finished arrow is a hundred and ten centimetres or more. The binding threads are held fast by a mixture of resin and beeswax, coloured with ochre in the case of new arrows.

I tried giving the Onges hooks and lines; they were intrigued by my demonstration of how to leave lines overnight and draw them in next morning loaded with fish, but no more. This was not superstition or fear of the unknown but sheer adherence to established custom. They have neither incantations, amulets nor propitiating

---

[1] Formerly made of *Tridacna*, or very hard wood. Some of the latter are still to be found, but all the other types of head – fish quills, bone, and *Tridacna* – have disappeared long ago.

signs to help them. Even the *marque de chasse* found on their arrow heads had no major significance; in all probability they merely served to indicate the best arrow and at most they served as a warning to the womenfolk not to touch them (it is interesting that I never saw any woman or child with a bow or an arrow). But this is as far as they go towards superstition, and its only effect is to enhance the division of duties between the sexes.

The Onges, unlike the Jarawas and Arioto, have never lost the art of canoe making, and the building of a new canoe is an important matter. The selected tree, always one of the three species of *Sterculia*, is felled and then hollowed out slowly and laboriously with a rudimentary form of hatchet, the work often being done by one man alone. The weight of the felled trunk makes it necessary for the work to be done where it falls, but after much patient whittling away the resulting canoe is extremely light, with thin walls, though still not light enough to be carried to the water, never far away. A series of short logs are used as rollers in the age-old way and the builder's friends all gather to help clear a way through the undergrowth and prepare the rollers. Only a few are needed; all is soon ready and the Onges watch delightedly as the canoe glides away down to the shore. These canoe-ways often provided me with an easy path to the sea if I came upon them in the forest. Sometimes they led not to shore but to one of the many creeks, where salt water and marine fauna penetrate miles inland and make it easy for the Onges to launch their canoes from a point far from the sea.

The Onge canoe, hollowed out in one piece, is a survival of the ancient canoes of the Neolithic age, found in Switzerland and elsewhere in Europe. It survives in the Andamans, and through Oceania to the Americas, in northern Asia (notably among the Ainu) in south-west Asia, and even in south-east Africa.

The canoe has no distinction between bow and stern, and is commonly navigated from either. At each end of the canoe a crude platform juts out, on which the harpoon throwers stand. Very careful attention is paid to the float, which is fragile, and is therefore kept on the lee side. The object of it is to prevent the canoe from capsizing, which it is otherwise very liable to do owing to its round keel, always left in the natural shape of the tree-trunk. I had some experiences of rough seas in one of these canoes

– I saw the float roll over my head and the entire contents of the canoe, men and cargo alike, rolled out into the water. The Onges regard this as a great joke; the canoe cannot sink, it is easily righted, and they have neither clothes nor baggage, so why worry? But even so, their canoes are far more stable in the water than any European-type craft of the same size.

When the sea is rough the Onges all move to the side of the canoe which carries the float and one lies out on the float itself to prevent it from rising out of the water as the trunk rolls. Very light waves will swamp the canoe, but it never sinks, as the float always remains on the surface, with the occupants of the canoe clinging to it. I had to do this myself on several occasions, while the Onges dived after all my baggage in great glee.

All over the world local craft are always the best adapted to local conditions. Several times I was able to land on Little Andaman in stormy weather only by leaving a modern sloop for the Onges' frail craft, identical with those in which they reached and spread over the archipelago in ancient times.

So important are their canoes to the Onges that they will expend what is for them an enormous amount of time and energy in choosing the right tree and removing the branches and the lianas twining round it. Then they wait with (for them) quite extraordinary patience for the scars to heal and become watertight before they fell the tree and begin the real work of making the canoe.

On Little Andaman the single outrigger canoe is the only craft used. On Great Andaman the Jarawas, who lost the art of canoe-building during their centuries of enforced hiding in the forests, only put together very primitive rafts, hastily constructed when they have to cross a creek or a river, and then abandoned on the far side to the termites.

These rafts are merely a number of tree-trunks laid side by side and bound together with lianas and *Ficus* bark. I have seen them lying abandoned on Middle Andaman and in 1938 one was taken by the police on the occasion of the capture of three Jarawa children. Extremely roughly made, these rafts are never taken out to sea, but in recent years they have been enough to encourage the spread of the Jarawas towards North Andaman.

Among the few surviving Negritos on North Sentinel the Onge

type of canoe is the only craft seen. I saw some hauled up on the beach, identical with the ones I had seen the Onges building, even to the *Nautilus* shell as a baler. In face of this and other evidence there can be little doubt that the people of North Sentinel are descended from the Onges, possibly driven off course by some storm, and then isolated on the island.

The Arioto, copying Indian and Burmese craft, have in recent times come to modify the original canoe somewhat, deepening the gunwales and doing away with the float. The result is a craft which though it remains small is unlikely to fill with water in heavy seas. But even the Arioto prefer the single outrigger canoe for sea voyages.

The only real seafarers, however, are the Onges, who make regular hunting trips as far as Rutland. In the past they sometimes made devastating raids as far as Car, but these have died out over the past hundred years as their numbers have dwindled. There is certainly no doubt that at one time the Onges undertook considerable sea voyages in canoes the same as they build today.

The work involved in the building of these canoes is, as I have said, enormous. The preparatory work on the tree, and then the felling, are hard enough without proper equipment. I gave my Onge friends some long-handled wood-cutter's axes, to help in this part of the work. In their enthusiasm they chopped so hard they soon broke the handles and chipped some of the tempered blades, so that I had to take them to Port Blair for repair! But the real work begins with the working of the felled trunk. Then a small and very crude form of hatchet[1] has to be used, flaking off small strips like a plane; fire is never used to assist in the process. Fortunately the *Sterculia* wood usually chosen is soft.

The original shape is not touched after the required length, calculated so as to allow for the harpoon-thrower's platform at each end, has been cut. The irregularities of the trunk are left intact, so that the canoes look distorted and even ugly despite their seaworthiness. During the preliminary stage of stripping the bark great care is taken not to chip the outer ring of wood immediately below the bark; this is smooth and fine-grained, and more waterproof than the inner layers. One danger is that as the wood dries

---

[1] The blades used to be made from *Tridacna* shell, but in more recent times they have come to be made of iron from wrecked ships cast up on the beaches.

out small cracks will open up and let water through the end of the canoe; these the Onges stop with resin.

Then comes the decision which side of the trunk is to be the keel. Once this has been decided, the upper surface is chipped flat and the hollowing out of the centre section begins, leaving the flat platform at each end. The finished shell is often no more than three centimetres in thickness, increasing slightly under the end platforms to protect the ends of the canoe as they grate on the reefs.

The float and booms, which project considerably, are for obvious reasons attached after the canoe has been rolled to the water. The booms are made of heavy hard wood, but the float itself, made of *Hibiscus tiliacus* or *Sterculia villosa*, has to be not only light, so as to float, but soft, so that the fixing pegs can be driven in easily. These are set into the float in a series of triangles, held in securely by the expansion of the wet wood and the upward force of the sea. The free ends of the pegs are then lashed together in groups of three so that each triangular set becomes a pyramid. The outrigger booms are set parallel to each other; each runs right across the hull, firmly lashed into holes bored on each side of the canoe high in the gunwales, and extends at least three metres out on one side. The apex of each pyramid formed by the float pegs is lashed up to one of the booms, holding the float fast to the booms above it.

The canoes have no reinforcing ribs either inside or out, and because of their inherent fragility they are never left in the water; they are dragged up over specially cleared runways to the communal huts near the shore. There they are left lying in the sun among the Ipomeas.

The direct heat dries them so rapidly that the wood invariably develops cracks, and the Onges resort patiently to their invariable remedy; resin is smeared over the cracks inside and out, and reinforced by a network of fibres laid on top, with a further layer of resin to seal them over.

Once on shore the canoes are left lying till they are next wanted, but with everything ready; the invaluable *Nautilus* is ready to bale out, so too are the point, cord and shaft of the harpoon, the large flat stones on which fire is carried without damaging the craft, and the blocks of wood to knock the harpoons out of the turtle shells.

I examined a number of canoes drawn up on the beach. They varied in size from some eight to ten metres long, built to carry twenty people, to small single-manned craft three to four metres long, and there were some very small ones clearly intended to encourage the children to set out on their own. The very large canoes are, however, rare. The beam also varied considerably from some barely wide enough to admit a man's knees to others of one and a half metres or more.[1]

In the shallows, contrary to some assertions, paddles are never used; the booms would make alternate paddling extremely difficult. Reversed harpoon shafts are instead used as punt poles and oars, usually made of *Myristica longifolia*, are used only in deep water. They are sometimes but not always lashed into the holes in the gunwale through which the booms pass. They are short, not more than 1·3 metres long and are always rowed forwards (obviously there would be a danger of stubbing a reef if the European style of rowing was used). Like the canoes, the oars vary somewhat in size. Very roughly made they consist of a handle ninety centimetres long and a forty-centimetre blade. The grip tapers almost to a point and increases gradually in diameter towards the blade, which is long, narrow, blunt-ended and flat-convex in section. Usually it is merely roughly shaped with the Onges' crude hatchet, but occasionally it is smoothed off with a sharp *Cyrena* shell. The helmsman and pilot stand on the two platforms, guiding the canoe with oars. As far as possible the rowers avoid the side bearing the outrigger mechanism; any deviation of course caused by the unilateral rowing is corrected by the two steersmen.

When they first launch a canoe the Onges decorate it with ochre designs like those on their bodies and the hollowed logs used to hold honey, although they are washed off as soon as the craft enters the water. As usual the men do all the work up to that point and the women do the painting. The initial painting is the only form of ornament on the canoes; there is not even a mark of ownership, although each canoe is curiously enough recognized as the property of one man, despite the fact that everyone has helped to

---

[1] I am unable to agree with Brown that the Onge canoes are extremely small, that they have bow and stern, and that their floats are inefficient. My own experiences of travelling in the canoes has led me to the opinion that on these and other points Brown was wrong, possibly partly because he never actually visited Little Andaman.

build it (when I wanted to acquire two for the new anthropological museum at Port Blair and the Indian Museum in Calcutta I had to bargain with the men recognized as the owners, although the price had to be distributed among all the members of the group).

The chief delight of the men on their fishing trips is the capture of a Giant Turtle. I have already described (p. 88) the spear harpoons which the Onges use to catch them. Once caught, the wretched animals are subjected to a form of vivisection utterly incomprehensible to the Western mind; they are literally cut up alive and the pieces thrown into the boiling cooking-pot. Nor have I ever witnessed anything so terrible as the way in which the Onges, in the absence of any suitable cooking vessel, or the materials for an earth oven, roast these turtles whole and alive over a slow fire. They seem totally unable to realize that animals can feel pain and laugh like children at the other atrocious tortures they unwittingly inflict not only on the turtles, but on every living thing that falls into their hands.

These marine turtles (as far as I was able to see there were no land turtles in the Andamans) yield a far greater amount of food than the dugong, and provide the islanders with both meat and eggs. Two species are common in the seas round the islands, *Chelonia virgata,* or the green turtle, and *Caretta imbricata,* which supplies the shells normally sold commercially. The Onges prefer the former, which are both meaty and more plentiful.

Turtle-hunting and egg-collecting is done by the menfolk. The method is very like that used for dugong and large fish, using the harpoon. Owing to their fear of the spirits abroad in the night, the Onges never go near the beaches between dusk and dawn, when it would be easy to take the turtles on land and immobilize them by turning them on their backs. They do know this trick, however, and use it when captured turtles (often weighing up to a hundredweight) are too heavy to carry in the canoe; the animals are turned on their backs and dumped on the beach ready to pick up later.

The Onges harpoon the turtles from canoes, preferably at night when the turtles are nearing the shore, which they never approach in the day time. When there is a moon the creatures are easily seen, and on dark nights the phosphorescence of the sea helps.

Once struck by the harpoon the turtle is trapped by the cord tied to the head of the harpoon while the shaft, detached by the blow, floats on the water till it is picked up. The target is large, the distance is short, and so the harpoon never fails.

The spirits of the night do not walk on the sea, so the turtle-hunting expeditions are all sea-borne, the canoes setting out to meet the turtles as they come in towards the shore to mate. When the moon is high the tropical seas are as clear as by day; on dark nights the resin torches carried in the canoes light the sea for a fair distance. Beyond their range, the turtles as they swim disturb tiny marine creatures, which promptly emit their phosphorescence, revealing clearly to the Onges the path of their unsuspecting victim.

These torches are about one metre long and fifteen centimetres in diameter, made of twisted palm leaves tightly bound with reed fibres. Inside is a carefully balanced mixture of resin and embers, which burns with a very bright flame. In recent years a variant has been introduced – huge lumps of gum were driven on to the shores of Little Andaman from some unknown distant shipwreck, and the Onges, having discovered how well the unknown substance burned, began mixing it with the embers in their torches. I can still see the Onges' child-like pleasure as they admired the effect of their new product, a gift, like their petrol-drum cooking-pots, from the sea.

Their torches for use on land are much smaller – about thirty centimetres long and ten centimetres in diameter, but made in exactly the same way. It is interesting that similar torches are found eastwards throughout Polynesia and are used everywhere in the same way for hunting turtles and their eggs from the same type of canoe.

The victim, struck as it comes to the top to breathe, disappears at once into the sea, dragging the cord with it. In less than ten minutes, however, it reappears on the surface and is hoisted aboard, often almost helping itself into the canoe with its thrashing flippers. Quite often turtles are caught while they are asleep on the surface, or mating, in which case the pair are easily captured. And in stormy weather, when the high seas make it difficult for them to negotiate the reefs back to the open water, the Onges can catch them and 'ride' them to the shore. I have seen the surviving Arioto do this, turning the turtle over on its back as soon as it is landed, and then blinding the wretched creature by putting both eyes out with a sharp stick, so that it cannot escape even if it manages to right itself.

Turtle eggs are easy to find. Before laying them in the sand about one metre deep, the turtle makes several visits about a fortnight beforehand to choose the spot. The huge footprints she leaves in the sand are easily seen, and watch is kept on the spot. When the Onges know roughly where to look they know that by poking in the sand with a stick they must in the end find the eggs. As one man, and happy as sandboys, they dig in the sand, lower and lower, till the sight of the first egg is greeted with a shout of triumph. One by one the eggs emerge to fill the baskets, hastily improvised and lined with great leaves.

The female may actually be seen depositing the eggs, up to two hundred at a time. Some will be infertile, and are smaller, with no yolk, but normally they are the size and shape of a billiard ball, deposited one after another at the rate of ten a minute. As they are laid a viscous secretion flows over them so that the sand sticks to them. As it dries, however, the sand can be rubbed off the shells, which are not rigid and resemble a shining white parchment; on each egg is a tiny round indentation, which increases in size within two or three days and makes the egg look as though it has shrivelled in the sun. In fact, the eggs will not hatch unless they remain buried deep in the sand.

Not more than half the turtle eggs laid in the Andamans hatch out into young turtles, so eager for them are man and beast alike. Man is their worst enemy, and it is no exaggeration to say that no clutch laid on Little Andaman has any hope of hatching. Man and animals alike range the beaches in search of the delicacy. First come the pigs, so greedy that if they come upon a female in the act of laying they give her no time even to cover the eggs. Then come the monitors, voracious lizards two metres long, and on the east coast near Nachuge, huge crocodiles as well. Finally, *Paradoxurus*, the wild cat of the Andamans, takes anything that is left.

The Onges have to compete with all these for turtle eggs, and they are nearly always too late. They have to look instead to the deserted islands, like the nearby South and North Brother. Here the young turtles have some chance of hatching, but as soon as they emerge from the eggs and make their way towards the sea, led by some unerring instinct, fresh predators are ready to pounce on them. Hungry gulls and fish, and the giant crabs, lie in wait and sometimes not one escapes.

But the annual survival of only ten young from each female would be enough to allay any fears for the extinction of the species and fortunately reproduction takes place several times a year, often four or five times, according to the Onges, mainly from March to September.

In the case of eggs which I protected and watched, incubation lasted sixty to seventy days depending on the time of year. During the whole of the incubation period the Onges regard them as edible, like the Bushmen of the Kalahari, whom I saw take and eat birds' eggs regardless of their age or state of development. The Onges even like the turtle embryos when cooked, and the other contents of the shell. Curiously enough, however long they are cooked the whites of turtle eggs never set, although the yolk does and is excellent. The Onges, as a sign of great respect, often gave me baskets full of the hard-boiled yolks.

Turtles, despite their peaceable appearance, are extremely agressive, and will take on nearly anything they meet. Their battles are one of the most amusing things in the animal world. The males of the marine turtles rarely approach the shore, except to fight each other. This they do ferociously, biting at everything within reach, regardless of being bitten themselves, as the land turtles do in the mating season. The aim is to overturn one's enemy so that he is quite helpless, after which the winner ambles off, leaving the vanquished to his own devices (the trick is to get one's head under one's opponent's body and lever upwards). A turtle, once on its back, takes hours to right itself, which it can only do by accident, when its frantic wriggling and beating in the air with its legs hollows the sand away underneath its back so that it flops over the right way up.

One of the Onges' greatest enemies in their search for food is the crocodile, *teboirona*, as they call it. They have no means of fighting the creature, so they limit themselves to fearing it and building stories round it. On Little Andaman crocodiles are found only near Nachuge on the west coast, in the deep waters of Jackson Creek, *To-ggue*. There used to be numbers of them in a few places on Great

Andaman, in Yeratil Jig (near Port Anson, about fifteen miles from Long Island) in Diglipur (or Dilyapur) Creek, near Port Cornwallis, and in Wilima Jig,[1] but they are now extinct. In March 1952 the Onges had described the presence of crocodiles so clearly to me as to leave no doubt what they meant, and I soon received confirmation when I found their tracks on the sand about one kilometre from the mouth of Jackson Creek, on the right bank, and then saw some lying on the shore across the creek. Through my field glasses I saw small birds pecking between the teeth of the great wide-open jaws. As we approached they slid lazily into the sea, some re-appearing a little later, their cavernous mouths rising vertically out of the water. Every day after that I saw them swimming quietly near the banks, and one afternoon my men and I between us saw over a dozen, near Nachuge, dozing in the mud or in the water.

The Onges assured me that crocodiles will come out of the water to a certain whistle. I got them to try it; the Onges whistled, and whistled again, but no crocodiles came!

Very different from the great turtles and the crocodiles, but equally important in the daily life of the Onges, are the crabs from which the islanders make their ancient and very characteristic pipes. They eat the crabs and use the claws to make the pipes, cutting them across the joint and boring a hole in the end, as they have done since time immemorial, to smoke aromatic leaves from the forest. Fragments of similar pipes, charred with use, appear in even the lowest strata of the kitchen-middens, dating back thousands of years and proving the antiquity of the smoking habit. Contrary to popular belief, smoking did not begin everywhere with the introduction of tobacco – in Asia at least men smoked thousands of years ago.

The claw pipes of the Onges have a groove cut round the end which goes into the mouth, so that the teeth can grip it better. I have seen identical pipes, with the same groove, in the Melville Islands, where there are many other signs of ethnographic connections with the Andamans. The canoes, for example, are identical with those of the Andamans; the peoples themselves, however, are today very different physically.

[1] According to Portman a man was dragged into the water here on 11 May 1894 by a crocodile and killed; several similar incidents have occurred since.

These crabs are enormous, weighing one and a half kilograms, and are very tasty. Like many land crabs they have one large claw and a smaller one, the difference being quite marked in the males, though hardly noticeable in females. Some appear left-handed, some right-handed; I confirmed this by looking at thousands of them with the help of my Indians, and sent some to the Institute of Zoology at the University of Genoa for further examination.

On the inside of the large claw, to hold the prey while the crab bites, are protuberances that look like teeth. They have a very similar function and are a good example of superficial similarity in different types of organs designed for a similar purpose.

The females, like those of other crabs, carry the mass of round, almost transparent, orange-coloured eggs under the abdomen, attached to her swimmerets and well protected. In the great crabs from which the Onges make their pipes the bluish-green shell is reflected on to the eggs, giving them a beautiful sheen. Immediately the young are hatched, they cling underneath the mother's abdomen like the eggs, so that if a female is caught one can be sure of having the whole brood. Even at this stage the sex and the disparity of the claws is discernible as the young are exact replicas of the adults. Two curious things about them are that the number of the two sexes in any brood are exactly equal, and that in the males there are equal numbers right- and left-handed. The point is an interesting one, and I hope geneticists will be able to investigate it further.

Another important feature in Onge life is the *Nautilus*, the cephalopod whose shells provide the only drinking vessels they know. *Nautilus* shells, unlike those of gastropods, are spiral in one plane, with interlocular septa. The mollusc occupies the last, or largest, of the whorls, which communicates with the rest of the spiral by a cylindrical syphuncle running through the mid-line of the shell. This is connected to the creature's viscera by a vascular tube, which for hydrostatic purposes regulates the amount of air and water in the chambers. Each chamber is concave on the side nearest the aperture, and the distance between the septa increases with the size of the whorls, to a fixed maximum, limited by their number, which is constant in adults. *Nautilus*, a living fossil from the time of the ammonites, is the last survivor of a genus dating from the Silurian period; long ago there were many species, although only four have been found since 1500. It is found only in the seas round Australia and Malaysia, flourishing round the Andamans, growing rarer towards Indonesia, and reaching as far as the Philippines.

Although *Nautilus* shells are very often thrown up by the sea on the shores of Little Andaman (though rarely whole, because they are so fragile), I never managed to find one alive. The creature prefers to live below thirty metres, where it can be taken with a hook and line. I distributed some to the Onges and offered them every possible inducement, but no one managed to catch a live *Nautilus*. The lovely shells are striped white and rosy pink on top, shading to a mother of pearl colour underneath, and when polished and shaped make beautiful cups or ornaments. I brought some back to Italy with me, but the best were stolen. In one collection in the Zoological Museum of the University of Florence there are some fine ones set in silver, now of considerable value.

Another shell which the Onges use is that of the huge bivalve *Tridacna*, the elephant of the mollusc world (see p. 114). For many hundreds of years they have filled these shells with water and used them as mirrors when they paint themselves. (The reflection is poor, however, and they fell enthusiastically on the mirrors I had taken with me. These they named *quietanga*, derived from their name for *Tridacna*, and followed me all over the island to get them.)

Two species of *Tridacna* are found on Little Andaman; *Tridacna gigas*, the larger, and *Tridacna squamosa*, large, but somewhat lighter in weight. Both live in relatively shallow water and are equally terrifying once they have got a hold (see p. 114). Fortunately, the Onges have learnt to surprise them when they are open and slash the single immensely powerful muscle, which closes the two halves of the shell. The flesh is edible when well boiled, and certain parts can even be quite tasty, with a delicate sea flavour; I even ate some raw, much to the horror of the Onges. (They were equally scandalized at my eating raw some of the excellent oysters, which they despise.)

Some of the *Tridacna* of the Andamans and Nicobar can weigh over two and a half hundredweights. The actual flesh is not heavy – the two halves of a magnificent *T. squamosa* that I caught at Nancowry in the Nicobars and gave to the Governor of the Andamans weighed nearly one and a half hundredweights and were over 1·3 metres in diameter. They are now used for the holy water in the new church of San Piero in Palco, in Florence, like those in the church of St Sulpice in Paris. Two valves of *T. gigas*, rather smaller, are being used for the same purpose in the church of Marco Polo in Viareggio.

Among the creatures the Onges hunt on the shores are crayfish, which can be taken in plenty in the streams of Little Andaman, although I found none on Great Andaman or in the Nicobars. As they were so common I assumed they were a known species and did not bother to collect any. In Madras, however, an expert on freshwater crustacea, Sri Sada Siva, told me that this appeared to be a new species and it would be well worth while returning to Little Andaman to collect further specimens, as the few I had brought are now lost. There are tens of thousands of them everywhere.

These freshwater crayfish are so tasty that they have entered into Onge folklore, and their tastiness is praised in song. They are baked on burning embers, without salt, as always, and just the charred shell is removed before they are eaten. The clean fresh water in which they live prevents any taint in the flavour. I must confess to having eaten them every day without realizing their importance as a possible new species. They are fairly large, about fifteen centimetres long, and almost black, in natural imitation of the dark rocks among which they try to vanish out of sight, although the Onges never fail to spot them. The males have slender pereiopods, with claws almost twice as long as the whole body; these the creatures thrust out before them, and so slender are they that it is difficult to catch a male with both pereiopods intact. After hatching, the young, which are identical with the adults as soon as they hatch and can therefore be sexed by the presence and absence of pereiopods, cling bunched together for several weeks, attached by their claws to their mother's swimmerets before making their way into the troubled waters of the rivers, where the great carp are waiting to prey on them.

Yet another freshwater creature eagerly sought by the Onges is one that is almost black in colour, a strange survival of some remote geological era. Like other members of the family it has no scales, and the mouth, armed with teeth, is not protractile. On Little Andaman I saw several specimens weighing over a kilogram, and many smaller ones, all good to eat. Near my base camp at Labanar, the men caught sackfuls of them, and I found young ones near the communal hut at Togalanghe.

There a rocky path winds down to the banks of the river Tciongarè (or Chongaree) to the south of the camp. In various places, where the path levels out, black muddy water collects into pools full of rotting leaves, lying on a bed of ooze and slime. In these pools, which appear and dry up again very quickly, I was surprised to catch a number of *silurides*. When it rains heavily, however, the pools link and join up with the river where the fish live, so that as the water disappears again any fish which have entered the pools are prevented from returning to the river, and are left lying in the slime as the water evaporates. These silurides have no gills, and are equipped instead with nostrils of an unusual type; from the nostrils protrude two cylindrical tubes, half a centimetre long in fish fifteen centimetres long, the same blackish colour as the rest of the body. The tail and the long dorsal fin are yellowish, and the long ventral fin running from the anus to the tail is whitish. There are two large lateral pectoral fins, with two very small ones between them. The eyes are large, starting out of the head like tiny glass domes. Very unfortunately a number of specimens which I had most carefully preserved were lost in transit from Port Blair to Calcutta, when some of my baggage, including the crabs and a collection of face masks of Nicobarese which had cost me a great deal of trouble, mysteriously disappeared *en route*.

The Onges do not eat eels,[1] which they regard as snakes, but they several times brought me examples of a very fine freshwater eel whose presence on Little Andaman I had not suspected. The Onges caught them, as they do all fish, with their bows and arrows. All weighed over half a kilogram and looked and tasted like European eels.

The eel of the Andamans, like those of Europe and America, has a long, almost cylindrical body and a single fin which begins on the back, circles the tail, and ends under the body just in front of the anus. There is also a pair of strong pectoral fins. The head distinguishes it from other eels, its rounded snout and wide mouth being

---

[1] The Arioto, however, eat eels, and also mice and other small animals, although food is given to them by the Governor in return for police duties. Brown also refers to the eating of snakes and mice on Great Andaman.

rather shorter than in other species, with rows of small teeth covering the palate. The jaws themselves, however, have only one row of teeth, all very pointed. To my intense annoyance, my eel specimens were lost with the silurides.

On rare occasions the Onges manage to catch the toad fish of the mangrove swamps. These curious little animals are apparently a compromise between the fish and the frog; they can breathe both in the air and under water and like to come out of the water to take a walk. They wriggle about in the pools left by the ebb tide, popping out into the air as soon as they meet anything suspicious, and hopping away over quite considerable distances. But normally they wander peacefully about on the mud, propelling themselves with their two pectoral fins, which are attached to the end of a form of arm. In size (never over twenty centimetres long) and colour they remind one of the gudgeon, to which they are related. They belong to the genus *Periophthalmus*, of the order Gobiidi. They seem to prefer living in the open rather than in the water, and appear to look forward to low tide, when the tiny creatures on which they feed are about. Hunger satisfied, they cling to some stone or tree-trunk, often in an almost vertical position, and will stay there over half an hour, particularly if their tail is touching the water, as this keeps their body damp and helps them to breathe by means of ingenious gill sacs filled with air.

Toad fish move into the marshes as the sea recedes and move back as the tide returns. In the middle of the day they seek the shade in the damp crevices of the mangrove swamps. They seem to glory in the first rays of the morning sun, their huge erectile eyes, which never rest, moving endlessly from side to side. Their independent movement enables the creature to gaze at the sun with one eye and look for likely prey with the other. The two eyes, set closely together on top of their flat heads make them look rather ridiculous. Another striking feature about them is a kind of sucker, or adhesive disc, formed by the ventral thoracic fins. These have a loose fold of skin on the back, so that when the fins are brought together in front of the body, the skin falls into a funnel shape, which when pressed against a stone or tree-trunk adheres to it by suction, holding the animal fast.

I was amused by the way toad fish can be domesticated as soon as they are caught. I kept some in my tent, leaving water available for them and feeding them on the table. As soon as they saw worms wriggling, they would move cautiously towards them and then snap them up like lightning. They became used to sitting in my hand quite undisturbed, looking round in two directions at once in an interested way. Flies held by the wings fascinated them more than anything, and they used to stare at the insects as though hoping to mesmerize them. They made delightful pets.

More prosaically, they are very good fried. Outside Little Andaman I found hundreds every day near Golpahar on Middle Andaman, and as the fish market in Port Blair was over a day's journey away we used many for non-scientific purposes.

Dugong, monitors, snakes, jungle cats, bats, leeches – all abound in Little Andaman and I had ample opportunities to study them. The dugong are well known to the Onges, but I only saw them at Bumila Creek (Cuateniabo) and Jackson Creek, where I did not have the time to catch any; the Onges tried, but without result.

Dugong (from the Malayan *Dyong*, introduced into scientific Latin as the family Dugongidae), are large mammals of the order *Sirenia*. They have a short fish-like body, with closeable nostrils above a cavernous mouth, which is surrounded by short bristly whiskers and armed with a brush-like, horny plate. In the male two short tusks hang down each side of the mouth, like a miniature hippopotamus, giving the animals a cumbersome, ugly look. The Onges prize the dugong, but rarely manage to capture one; when they do, there is great feasting. I was never able to try it, or even acquire any really close observations of the creatures.

Monitors or dragon-lizards, on the other hand were under my feet every day, although the islanders never eat them. I used to put out as bait fish or pig carcasses rejected by the Onges as being too lean, and we could then shoot as many as we wanted as they rushed to the bait from all sides. I collected their skins for various museums, using the carcasses as further bait.

The Andamanese variety is well known and it closely resembles *Varanus niloticus*, the Nile monitor, to which it is related. The largest can be two metres long, including the long, very tapering tail. As they approach their prey, sniffing at it, their forked tongue, twice the length of the head, flashes in and out of its sheath with incredible speed. Although they have strong legs they move slowly and it is easy to catch them by the tail, providing one takes care to avoid being bitten, and one blow on the spine kills them. Compared with the turtle, for example, their vitality is poor, and they die very quickly, although strangely enough the heart beats for some hours after death.[1]

These carnivorous lizards are the jackals of the Andamans, scavengers ready to eat anything, from offal even the dogs will not eat to the rotting carcasses of the dogs themselves, and even of their own kind. In the forests of the Andamans death is swift and silent, and the monitors ensure that it leaves no trace.

---

[1] On a number of occasions I took out the respiratory and digestive system, with the heart, and both systole and diastole and peristalsis continued regularly for some hours.

CHAPTER SEVEN

The Unity of the Negritos

It appears that the Andamanese, before their migration to the archipelago, copied from other Asiatic and Oceanic peoples customs and rites whose origin and meaning were unknown to them. They went on and on observing these rites blindly, till they gradually degenerated to their present rudimentary form. In the Onges of today they seem like mere superstitions, badly digested importations, far from any of their original meaning. The process is a phenomenon which has occurred over and over again among primitive peoples who come in contact with other, to their eyes superior, cultures. They feel an urge to imitate something, as it were, more elegant, and so come to follow the new ways out of habit. I have seen the effects of this both in Africa and in Asia, particularly as the result of contact with European influences.

The practice of vivisecting animals for food, for instance, was widespread throughout the world, frequently in connection with certain ideologies, although these were not usually based on pure superstition. Rituals which to us are horrible beyond measure are seen by primitive peoples from childhood merely as a necessary part of cooking or the acquisition of food. And yet such practices are found also in peoples with a culture considerably beyond the primitive. Some cannibals, for example, are relatively advanced; there are in fact some cannibal peoples who have reached the stage of agriculture. The Andamanese, however, are far behind that stage of development, and they have never acquired the ideologies leading to cannibalism. One can only accept that they do genuinely believe that in practising vivisection they are acting for the common and the individual good.

There is an established and closely observed order of precedence

136

in the division of all meat. Certain cuts are the property of the hunter, of his helpers, and of his relations and after them, in order, of the remaining members of the group; everyone knows his position in advance. Each portion is tied round with a reed fibre, which is allowed to dangle out over the top of the communal cooking-pot ready to haul the meat out when required.

In the case of pork the prized cut is one which comprises the kidneys and the surrounding fat; this fat is called *cian*,[1] and is very highly esteemed. Some authors (Brown, for example) have stated that turtles and pigs are always cut up with the head ritually pointing towards the sea as otherwise the meat would be considered inedible. This is certainly not the case on Little Andaman, and I have never seen any such directional ritual among any of the Negritos, all of whom practise division of meat according to a prescribed order of precedence. Turtles at any rate are slaughtered facing up the sloping beach simply because it is then easier to hold the beast from behind and avoid its bite. Ritual there is, but usually with a good practical basis.

More ritual attaches to the way in which the game is carried back to the camp, and the wood to be used for the cooking fire. Pigs, killed and gutted, are tied in ropes made of *Ficus laccifera* and carried somehow on the back of the victorious hunter. If it is not far to the camp he will not bother to tie up the snout and feet, but otherwise the front and back legs are tied, and one long cord joins both pairs to the snout – again a practical ritual, giving the hunter a more compact weight to carry.

Man, Portman, Brown and others all say that each type of game has to be cooked over a fire of a particular wood. My own observations showed that whereas the ritual of dissection is inviolable, the Onges always use the first wood that comes to hand, regardless of its source, taking as usual the line of least resistance. This is again in keeping with the tendency of primitive peoples to expend only the very minimum of energy to achieve their object. Their religious beliefs and superstitions are not carried to the limit, simply because

[1] It is interesting that in their very restricted world the Onges have few standards of comparison or words to express condemnation or approval, and this word *cian* is used as one of high praise, applied to inanimate objects, animals, and people alike. The precise qualities which are conveyed by the word are difficult to evaluate in the absence of fuller knowledge of the Onge language.

their love of existing with as little effort as possible is paramount. Since any wood is as good as the next for making a fire, the spirits conveniently have nothing to say in the matter. In other circumstances material considerations lead to quite the opposite effect: when the Onges dig up roots or tubers they not only replace the earth, but cover the place with leaves, the ritual having the good practical objective of appeasing the spirits and ensuring further supplies.

The preservation of skulls for magical purposes or out of pure superstition survives mainly in Asia and Oceania. In Asia it coincides with other beliefs which demand the killing of domestic animals by strangulation. I have seen this practised along the high reaches of the valley of the Brahmaputra, particularly among the Abor, and the Nagas, and in many other tribes to the south of Tibet and China, all of whom preserve skulls. Head-hunting, found throughout southern Asia, in the islands, and as far as Oceania, is also practised in the areas where animal skulls are preserved.

The preservation of animal skulls, particularly bear skulls, is still practised in mongoloid peoples as far as the north of Asia; apart from the Andamans and the Nicobars, human and animal bones are preserved in many parts of Indonesia and as far as New Guinea. In the corona of small islands along the west coast of Sumatra the custom coincides with many others, as well as with certain types of huts and canoes, all present in the Andamans and Nicobars. A good example are the huts raised up off the ground on stilts, common in the Nicobars, Nias, Engano, Mentawai and various parts of Indonesia. The single-boom canoes of these areas, quite apart from their general similarity of structure, all have certain identical features, even to the method of fixing the lateral float of green wood, with pointed hardwood pegs stuck in it like spills. This, again, cannot be due to chance; it must be the effect of a very ancient cultural diffusion, now surviving only in a few specific areas.

The skulls preserved by the Onges have one point of interest; it is the duty of the wife to clean the trophies brought back by her proud husband and then paint them lovingly with lines of ochre. After every successful hunting expedition the wives can be seen busily painting, while the husbands look on with satisfaction.

Brown states that dugong skulls are found among the hunting trophies of the Andamanese. I can myself vouch for the fact that this is not the case among the Onges or the twenty-three surviving Arioto; both keep dugong jaws and long bones, but the skulls of only pigs and turtles. The Andamanese in general do not regard animal bones as having the same protective powers as human; the existence in the Andamans of any magical practices connected with either animal or human bones has not, in my view, been adequately proved. In the absence of such proof I feel unable to agree with the authors who assert that these practices do exist, and I am inclined to feel that the cultural level of the peoples of the Andamans is so low as to rule out the existence of magic or witchcraft in any form.

From the mass of data of all kinds I was able to collect on my trips to the Andamans, a general pattern emerges from which it is possible to draw substantial conclusions as to the cultural and somatic origins of the Onges and hence of the other peoples of the archipelago. To summarize these conclusions must inevitably involve some repetition of what has been said in previous chapters.

Taking first the people of the Nicobar Islands, the nearest geographically to the Andamanese, it is generally accepted that with the exception of the Shom-Pen of Great Nicobar the Nicobarese are culturally closely similar. Although there are no pure Negrito types in the Nicobars there are evident crosses, similar to those which appear in one area of Sumatra to the east, where a small Negrito component exists among a predominantly mongoloid type. This may well be the result of the Negritos having spread at one time over a very wide area and there is in fact cultural evidence in support of the suggestion.

The mongoloid somatic type of the Nicobars appears in the general shape and proportions of the body, skin colour, facial contours, and the hair, which is long and straight, unlike that of the Negritos. Both types, however, have scant body hair, and differ in this respect from the pygmies of Africa.

Although the size and skin colour of most Nicobarese is very different from the Onges, a few are strikingly like them in facial contours, size, and woolly hair. There are also legends of a people who lived in the Nicobars long ago, small, very black, with tight curly hair; on Car Nicobar I was taken to a cave[1] where these people are said to have lived. The ethnographical evidence is such that there may well be some truth in the legend. The close similarity in detail, even identity, of the Onge and Nicobar canoes, and spiralled pottery, the presence in the wild state of the pig – the sum of this and other evidence cannot be overlooked. Car would have been the last point before the Andamans in the Negrito advance from the east. They would have remained on Car for a long time before moving on to the Andamans, and since Car is a completely flat coral deposit, with no true stone at all, it may be assumed that it was during their sojourn on Car that the Negritos lost the art of working it; this would explain the complete absence of stone implements in the Andamans.

The Negritos would thus have occupied the Nicobars before the mongoloids, and were then, as the somatic evidence shows, partially absorbed, or moved on to the Andamans. The burial customs and superstitions of the Andamanese reflect Nicobar influence with disinterment, reburial and retention of certain bones; such customs are also found sporadically in Oceania. Ritual governing hunting trophies is also very similar, as are weapons. The three-pointed arrow was found in both the Nicobars and the Andamans until comparatively recently; the Onges have none now, but their descendants – the Sentinellese and Jarawas – still used them very recently. Both the Nicobarese and the peoples of the Andamans (also various peoples in Indonesia and Oceania) cook without any form of salt. This is also the case in certain islands of the west coast of Sumatra, where there are also other similarities from huts to

[1] On 20 April 1952, I visited this cave with Sri B. S. Cengappa, head of the 1952 Nicobar Expedition; in the report of the expedition he did me the honour of naming the cave 'Cipriani Cave'. A schoolmaster on Car Nicobar told me of other caves in the archipelago, which had similar traditions of occupation in very ancient times. One facing the sea on the east coast of Catcial, one of the Nancowry group, was of considerable size, about a hundred metres long and fifteen metres high, and wider, its floor covered in a layer of guano. The same guano covered the floor of Cipriani Cave, which lies in a coral formation little more than ten metres above present sea-level. It has two openings, diametrically opposite and thirty-five metres apart. The cave consists of a wide central chamber, about seven metres in diameter, with many stalactites and stalagmites. Fortunately none of the archaeological deposit was damaged by the Japanese occupation and the traditions attached to the cave remain alive among the Nicobarese. It would need at least ten men working for at least six months to investigate the cave properly, but I am sure that the results would amply justify the cost of such an expedition.

head ornaments and religious ceremonies. In Oceania there is, too, the habit of changing personal names from time to time so prevalent among the Onges, and the existence of actual linguistic connections between Nicobarese, Andamanese, Semang, Aetà and peoples of Oceania have been demonstrated by experts.

Any differences which exist today are the result of centuries of contact with other peoples which the Semang and Aetà have experienced, unlike the Andamanese, who thus represent today the true Negritos. While life generally has changed somewhat over the centuries for the Semang and Aetà, certain typical facets of their culture have remained unaltered. Ritual cutting and distributing of game, the use of the arrow harpoon (always unfeathered) and the simple Onge-Negrito bow are still the same, despite the fact that the three groups have been separated for a very long time. Even the very absence of defensive weapons is a common feature; admittedly outside the Andamans arrows are poisoned and some may be feathered, but this is a recent and imitative innovation which is not found among the Andamanese, by virtue of their constant isolation. The persistence among the Onges of the simple bow tends to support the idea of Little Andaman as the first stage in the northward spread of the Negritos after they reached the island from Sumatra via the Nicobars. In Malacca the Semang have retained the same bow, as have the Aetà in the Philippines.

Among what may be termed similarities of physical habits is nose-rubbing as a sign of affection, found in the Andamans, in Oceania, and parts of Papuasia and Melanesia. In all these areas there is the same belief that pregnancy is due to entry of a spirit into the body, and the same habit of suckling children for as long as four years. Similar too throughout the area are the methods of 'curing' disease, such as smearing with ochre and heavy massage carried out beside a fire, swallowing of balls of ochre, and the 'smoking' of wounds, smeared with a mixture of ochre and honey. As protection from the sun or the rains (especially for the young children) crude umbrellas are made from giant palm leaves.

There are no prayers or propitiatory sacrifices to ensure health and well being, but there is throughout the area the same concept of mysterious forces to be feared, evaded, or let loose against enemies – never loved. Generally they are thought of in terms of spirits, usually active at night. There is some divergence in the way in which the spirits are invoked against enemies, involving the use of some personal possession – an example is the invariable destruction of the used *naquineghe*, or of hair after shaving. The same fear of the night induced by the idea of spirits walking abroad led to the making of torches from rolled palm leaves containing a mixture of embers and resin.

From the Andamans to Oceania the chief spirit is generally imagined in the form of a giant lizard, living at the top of the sky and ruling the storms; none of the peoples who believe in him ever eat any lizard or lizard-like creature. All of them have the same sexually suggestive dances, both male and female, sometimes inspired by the monitor or dragon-lizard, symbol of desire, and often associated with miming and dramatic representations of real and imaginary scenes. These dances, with their *joie de vivre*, are accompanied by the smoking of aromatic leaves in pipes which are frequently made from natural objects such as the claws of crustacea. The Onges in fact have since very ancient times used only this type as shown in the lower levels of the kitchen-middens dating back at least five thousand years. Everywhere, pipes of this kind are used indiscriminately by both sexes, passing from mouth to mouth. Pipes identical in every way with those of the Onges are found to the east of the archipelago, well into Oceania, and I have myself also seen them on Melville Island, north of Australia, always with the same notches for the teeth to grip. This undeniable evidence of the spread of identical pipes over so wide an area long before the possibility of European contacts cannot in my opinion be attributed other than to migration over vast distances in very ancient times.

Similar coincidences apply in the case of the arrow harpoon and indeed harpoons in general. I cannot agree with Brown in his assertion that the harpoon dates from the arrival of European influences, which brought the use of iron; the harpoon points made by long and patient working of *Tridacna* shells which I found in the kitchen-middens of the Andamans are in my view enough to refute the theory.

The canoes from which these harpoons are used, with the absence of distinction between bow and stern and the single float on the lee side, are extremely typical. They are identical in peoples which have been widely separated for a very long time and appear not only on the Andamans, and as far as Oceania, but also in North

Queensland and (as the Cape Bedford type) elsewhere. Oars, method of fixing the booms and float – all are similar throughout the area, including the Andamans.

Even game, once caught, is treated and distributed similarly by these peoples, from the Andamans to Oceania. Cooking is done without salt, in earth ovens (whether or not fire or red-hot stones are used) very different from those of Africa and America. The Semang and Aetà of today know how to make fire by friction, as do the peoples of New Guinea, Australia and Polynesia; the Tasmans also have the knowledge to do so, but prefer to carry burning logs with them on their journeys, like the Andamanese. In certain parts of New Guinea and perhaps in some of the Pacific islands (as in the Andamans) the art of fire-making was unknown or possibly forgotten until recent times; it is said that the Papuans of the Bay of Astralobius knew nothing of the art until the middle of the nineteenth century. But the only sure information comes from the Andamans, where, whether through ignorance or loss of knowledge, the art of fire-making is unknown and fire is always carried everywhere.

Among the objects typical of the Andamans and found also among the Semang, the Aetà, and other Oceanic peoples are the digging stick and the crude hatchet. The former, used for gathering edible roots and tubers, is merely a pointed stick, but every family possesses one. The hatchet is slightly more elaborate, having both handle and blade, and like the digging stick, occurs always in virtually the same form.[1] Objects woven from vegetable fibres are also very similar in appearance – often very durable and sometimes pleasing by any standards. In some places woven breast-plates are used in warfare, but here the Jarawas differ, using single sheets of bark.

These are but a few of the many examples which one can find of this striking similarity between these widely separated peoples. And alongside cultural similarities there exist others, anthropological and physical, which cannot be overlooked. Physically the

---

[1] This is simply a cutting tool fixed into a natural elbow in a suitable branch. The blade is fixed into the wood near the elbow, and the branch is cut off, so as to leave a short handle. The whole thing is reminiscent of a swan's head on a long neck, and is easily turned into a crude plane or adze by revolving the blade in the haft through a right angle.

most striking of these is ambidexterity. This is the general rule in the Onges and also appears as a normal trait in the primitive peoples of Oceania, America and Asia. Another physical characteristic of the Onges, reported also in Tasmans and various peoples of Oceania, is the early onset of ageing in both sexes; in the Tasmans the women are rarely fertile after the age of thirty, and this is also probably the case with the Onges. Unlike the Tasmans, however, the Onges, though sharing their very black skin colour, have among other physical differences markedly scant body hair. A study of their blood groups by Dr H. Lehmann (see also Mourant) has moreover lent very considerable support to the external physical evidence in favour of a relationship between the Andamanese and the people of Oceania, both past and present.

From the anthropological point of view perhaps the most outstanding feature of all these peoples is that despite their extreme aggressiveness towards outsiders their corporate sense is such that they have no need of leaders to give orders. Rarely are there hereditary leaders; such as they are, their leaders are chosen on the basis of outstanding powers, such as supposed clairvoyance, as in the Andamanese.

The Andamanese themselves know nothing of their origins, lost in the mists of time, and it is for us to trace them, working back along the paths cleared by the anthropologist, the ethnographer and the archaeologist. They represent today the survival, almost unchanged, of a culture once to be found all over Oceania, spread thousands of years ago by canoes hardly different from those the Onges use today. They carried the unknown seamen from island to island, bearing with them a way of life which in the Andamans at least was never to change – a point of arrival, rather than of departure. Driven in on themselves by circumstances of geography just as other circumstances now unknown had driven them there originally, they have remained isolated, dwindling in numbers over the centuries, until they were discovered by the modern world. Their reception of outsiders, however they come and whoever they may be, is aggressive; consciously or unconsciously the Andamanese seek to preserve the only way of life they know. And who can be sure they are wrong?

No one could deny the demographic decadence of the islanders, a prelude, if the process remains unchecked, to imminent extinction. But in the light of present knowledge it can be checked and perhaps brought to a halt. The resurgence of many peoples following the influx of new blood is an observed fact, and it may not be purely Utopian wishful thinking to hope that something of the sort may happen to the peoples of the Andamans. While the civilized world expresses horror at the idea of animal species becoming extinct, it does not seem to have any thought for human beings facing the same fate – surely humanitarian considerations, quite apart from any scientific notions, urge that action should be taken before it is too late?

References

MOUNT, F. J. *Adventures and Researches among the Andaman Islanders*, London 1863.

MOURANT, A. E. *The distribution of the human blood groups*, Oxford 1954.

PORTMAN, M. V. *A history of our relations with the Andamanese*, Calcutta 1899 (2 vols.).

RADCLIFFE-BROWN, A. R. *The Andaman Islanders*, 1948 (2nd edition).

Appendix

Below is given a brief summary of the evidence which in the author's opinion supports his view that the culture of the Andaman Islanders dates back at least to the Palaeolithic era.

I ABSENCE OF STONE IMPLEMENTS

There are in the Andamans abundant sources of stones suitable for shaping into tools. Despite this I found no traces whatever of any stone implements even in the lowest strata of the kitchen-middens, nor is there any evidence of their being used either in the more recent past or at the present time. Until the very recent introduction of iron the Onges always (as the kitchen-middens confirm) made tools solely of wood, with the addition of parts made from *Tridacna* shells, shaped by long and patient rubbing against stone. The only objects remotely approaching the definition of stone implements are the splinters of quartz or obsidian which are carried in the hair, and used as razors or, in the Arioto only, for primitive tattooing. These splinters, which are in no way shaped after being broken off, are thrown away as soon as they become blunt, and a new piece of quartz is crudely struck from a lump, by men or women indiscriminately. The existence of this one stone implement does not, in my view, justify the classification of the Onges (or the Andamanese in general) as a true Palaeolithic people; it would be more reasonable to class them as pre-lithic.

2 ABSENCE OF METAL WORKING

Even today the Onges' knowledge of metal working is confined to rubbing pieces of iron against stone to reduce them to the required shape. They have no knowledge of how to forge it, nor have they the tools to do so. Iron is clearly a very recent introduction, the importance of which the islanders, in the absence of any means of working it, have not fully realized.

3 IGNORANCE OF FIRE

The islanders' present ignorance of fire-making may possibly be the result of cultural decline, but this is not certain. In the presence of the considerable additional evidence in favour of the antiquity of the Andamanese culture it is, however, more likely that it is genuine ignorance, persisting in a pre-lithic people.

4 ABSENCE OF SALT

Although there can be no proof, it can be reasonably postulated that very primitive Man had no salt, and that in the Andamans this ignorance has persisted over thousands of years, owing to strict isolation. It is unlikely that the use of salt would have been completely lost, had it ever been ntroduced.

5 PRIMITIVE METHODS OF COOKING

Apart from the accidental and very recent introduction of petrol-drum cooking, the Andamanese use only the most primitive form of earth oven. This method of cooking was certainly known in the Palaeolithic era; at the entrance to the well-known Barma Grande cave near Mentone I have myself seen in the basal layers a number of stones bearing the marks of fire, too numerous merely to have formed some sort of hearth, and clearly not used to support cooking-pots, as Palaeolithic Man had none which would have withstood heat. The form of earth oven still used throughout the Andamans is undoubtedly of extreme antiquity.

6 FOOD VESSELS

The people of the Andamans still use for honey hollowed-out logs simiar to those seen in Palaeolithic wall paintings, which also depict baskets very like those still in use throughout the archipelago. The art of basket-making can be traced back at least to the later Palaeolithic era.

7 USE OF POTTERY

As with the other Negrito peoples, pottery was unknown in the earliest culture of the Andamans. Its appearance seems from the evidence of the kitchen-middens to have been contemporaneous with the introduction of the pig, i.e. to have been introduced by outsiders. It would be possible, using radio carbon methods, to calculate this date more accurately, but on purely archaeological evidence the introduction of pottery would appear to have occurred some five thousand years ago.

8 ABSENCE OF CANNIBALISM

If we may accept the evidence of the kitchen-middens, there has never at any time been cannibalism in the Andamans, although the practice certainly existed in the later Palaeolithic era; the Andamanese must thus have been isolated in the archipelago long before the practice became widespread.

9 DRINK

The Andamanese ignorance of any drink other than water may be regarded as additional evidence of the great antiquity of their culture.

10 ABSENCE OF CLOTHING

The Jarawas of both sexes have always remained completely naked. The Onges have only in comparatively recent times adopted a form of genital covering for their womenfolk; this custom has spread as far as the north of Great Andaman, and it seems probable that the separation of the Jarawas from the Onges dates from this time.

11 ABSENCE OF TATTOOING

All primitive peoples who are habitually completely naked adorn the body in some way. The Onges have never progressed beyond the early stage of painting themselves with ochre, and do not tattoo. Their sole ornaments are small necklaces of tusk shells, strips of bark, and sometimes flowers. In all this they resemble the Tasmans (see, however, p. 143 for certain important differences), who seem to have remained in an equally early stage of cultural development.

12 TOTEMISM AND THE CLAN

Here again the complete absence of any traces appears to indicate isolation before the spread of these very ancient concepts. Neither the Onges nor the Jarawas have ever progressed beyond the stage of independent groups of families. There is some spontaneous recognition of individuals as 'headmen' as a result of some generally accepted superiority of physique or discernment, but the concept goes no further than the giving of some weight to their views within the group.

13 MARRIAGE

The Onges are monogamous, like all peoples who have never progressed beyond the stage of hunting and gathering, and adultery is virtually unknown. Marriage consists merely of the man taking possession of the woman in the presence of the rest of the group, taking her by the hand to a new bed built for the occasion and allotted a place within the circle. The 'marriage' takes place in the late evening and is followed by frenzied dancing all night long by the light of the resin torches. The total absence of any form of ritual leads one to suppose isolation from a very early date indeed, but this cannot be more than conjecture.

14 BURIAL

The custom of burying the dead in caves still occupied by the living apparently existed in the Palaeolithic era. The practice has continued to the present time in the Andamans, where the dead are still buried under the family bed in the communal hut. It is known from Palaeolithic burials that even in that era objects were sometimes buried with the dead, and it is thus possible that the culture of the Andamans dates back to very early times.

15 EXHUMATION AND SECOND BURIAL

The custom of exhuming the bones of the dead and re-interring them after coloration (in this case with ochre) dates from the Palaeolithic era.

16 BONE NECKLACES

The custom of wearing necklaces of carpals, tarsals, phalanges and fragments of rib, is of extreme antiquity, and apart from the Andamans, has virtually disappeared.

17 RELIGION

There is evidence that even in Palaeolithic times there existed a belief in the survival of the spirit after death, and a fear of its return (hence the dead were buried securely bound in a knee-to-chest position, still the custom among the Andamanese). The Onges go no further than this and the idea of a Lord of the Spirits who rules all things, although on Great Andaman there has been some progress towards more anthropomorphic concepts. The complete absence of any form of cult, prayer, representation, or votive offering cannot, I feel, be the result of cultural decline from a more advanced age; this would have resulted in gross distortion and illogical superstition, but not in complete absence of any 'religious' practices of any kind.

18 SACRIFICE

No sacrifices of any kind are practised in the Andamans, nor is there any concept of propitiation, although there is evidence that even in the late Palaeolithic era some form of ritual sacrifice was practised, at least in Europe and probably over a much wider area. One would assume from this, and from paragraph 17 above, that the Andamanese is an even older culture.

19 TABOOS

Although my own experiences among the Onges have led me to think that taboos do not exist, some authors have asserted (in my view wrongly) their existence on Great Andaman. It is not, however, possible to draw any reliable conclusions on this point.

20 CEREMONIAL

The complete absence of any form of ritual surrounding birth, the purification of women, initiation, etc., or evidence of any such ritual in the past, is striking, in view of the prevalence in all the surrounding areas of strictly observed ceremonial for many occasions. As in the case of religion, such complete absence can only mean that the Andamanese became isolated before the idea of ritual spread to the area.

21 MEASUREMENT

The Andamanese have no means of counting, and no words to express gradations of time or size; to them everything is either 'small' or 'big'. They take no interest in the passing of years, and have no idea of their own age. To them life is but the passing of the seasons and the harvests of game and fish and fruits that they bring. This utter lack of any sense or form of numerical evaluation is further support for the extremely low stage of cultural development at which they became isolated.

22 ART

When painting their bodies with ochre the Onges have no idea of symbolic representation, and use only geometrical designs. These invariably seem spontaneous, and in my view do not represent a degenerate form of some more highly evolved art, half forgotten over the centuries; in short, the 'artists' of the Andamans, with no conception of symbolism, are even today less advanced than their Palaeolithic counterparts.

23 DIGGING STICKS

In late Palaeolithic deposits, stones with holes in them have been found which correspond to those still in use among peoples such as the Bushmen, to add weight to their digging sticks. The absence even today of any form of weighted stick in the Andamans, where stone is plentiful would appear to antedate the culture at least to early Palaeolithic.

24 HUNTING

The Onges still use the Palaeolithic throwing stick, although it is not their main hunting weapon. They have no idea of fixed traps, which must from the evidence have been known in Palaeolithic times, and it is hard to believe that a people so dependent upon hunting would have lost the art once it had been acquired. They have crude nets which the women use for fishing, but these are probably a comparatively recent introduction, which has arrived via the Nicobars.

25 DOMESTIC ANIMALS

The Andamanese have none, and this would seem to add weight to the evidence for their great antiquity.

26 ECONOMY

There is no economic system of any kind, and from the evidence available it is highly unlikely that even the most primitive form ever existed. There is no conception whatever of providing for tomorrow, or of any form of exchange or barter.

27 WEAPONS

The wall paintings of the Palaeolithic era depict bows and arrows, the former of both the simple and the double-curve type, and the latter with one or more points, similar to those still used in the Andamans. (The same *marques de chasse* as those found on bone arrowheads of the late Palaeolithic era were on *Tridacna* arrowheads which I found in the lower strata of the kitchen-middens.) The harpoon, with detachable point and cord, was widespread in the late Palaeolithic era, and this too has persisted unchanged to the present day in the Andamans.

28 NAVIGATION

There is no proof that Palaeolithic Man travelled by water, but it can be argued that the proven antiquity of the Andamanese culture is of itself evidence in favour of the supposition that he did.

The author is of the opinion that the sum of the evidence outlined above is overwhelmingly in favour of the continuing existence in the Andamans of what may well be a virtually unchanged Palaeolithic or even pre-lithic culture.

Index

Abor, 17
Aetà, 11–12, 36, 56, 74, 83, 85, 87,
    91–4, 141, 143
Adoption, 63–4
African pygmies, *see* Negrillos
Agriculture, 36–7
Albinos, 15
Alcohol, 5, 46
Alexander, T. E., 9
Amphibia, 37, 48, 70, 108, 112,
    133
Anadendron, 85
Ancestral spirits, 44
Andaman and Nicobar Gazette, 90 n.
Andaman archipelago, 1–2, 11,
    24–5, 28, 86, 112; *see also* Great
    and Little Andaman, Brother,
    Rutland and Sentinel Islands
Andamanese, 3, 11, 13, 16, 22–3,
    35–6, 136–45; *see also* Arioto,
    Jarawas and Onges
Angaman, 3
Anthropology, 11 ff., 63, 139 ff.
Ants, 95–8
Arak, 101
Arioto, 2–7, 13, 17, 23, 36, 45, 62–8,
    75–6, 78, 80–1, 84, 86–9, 91, 121,
    125, 132, 139, 147
Art, 39, 66, 74, 123, 152; *see also*
    Body painting
Artocarpus communis, 31
Asiatic pygmies, *see* Negritos
Axes, 93, 121, 123, 143

Balawa, 5
Bamboo, 56, 60, 86
Basket-making, 39, 93–4, 148
Bea, 5
Bees, 100–4
Beniaboì, 56, 59
Berié-Abdalù, 52, 69, 106
Betel, 101
Birds, 33, 37, 45, 70, 92, 101, 108–12
Blagden, 38
Bluff I., 8
Body painting, 22, 54, 67, 149, 152
Body temperature, 20
Bogig-iab, 5
Bone necklaces, 44, 76, 150
Bonington, 7
Bows and arrows, 83–6, 93, 118–19,
    132, 141, 153
Bregmatic furrow, 17
Brother Is., 18, 126
Brown, A. R., 44, 56, 79, 88, 92,
    104 n., 132, 137, 142
Bugheneh, 36
Bulundanghe, 31, 40–1
Bumila creek, 56, 134
Burial, 44, 66, 75–9, 140, 150
Burmese, 13, 46
Bushmen, 16–22, 127, 152
Butler Bay, 24
Butterflies, 107

Cadel, 9 n.
Cai, 11

155

INDEX

DATE DUE

FEB 2 1969			